STORIES OF GEORGIA

BY

JOEL CHANDLER HARRIS

Cherokee Publishing Company
Atlanta, Georgia

Library of Congress Cataloging-in-Publication Data

Harris, Joel Chandler, 1848-1908.
    Stories of Georgia.

    Originally published; New York; American Book Co., 1896.

    1. Georgia — History — Addresses, essays, lectures.
I. Title.
F286.5.H33   1985   975.8   85-25490
ISBN 0-87797-018-1 (alk. paper)

Originally published
New York, 1895

This book is printed on acid-free paper which comforms to the American
National Standard Z39.48-1984 *Permanence of Paper for Printed
Library Materials.* Paper that conforms to this standard's requirements
for pH, alkaline reserve and freedom from groundwood is anticipated to
last several hundred years without significant deterioration under normal
library use and storage conditions. ⊗

Manufactured in the United States of America

ISBN: 978-0-87797-018-7 Hardcover
ISBN: 978-0-87797-320-1 Paper

CHEROKEE PUBLISHING COMPANY
P.O. Box 1730
Marietta, Georgia 30061

PREFACE.

In preparing the pages that follow, the writer has had in view the desirability of familiarizing the youth of Georgia with the salient facts of the State's history in a way that shall make the further study of that history a delight instead of a task. The ground has been gone over before by various writers, but the narratives that are here retold, and the characterizations that are here attempted, have not been brought together heretofore. They lie wide apart in volumes that are little known and out of print.

The stories and the characterizations have been grouped together so as to form a series of connecting links in the rise and progress of Georgia; yet it must not be forgotten that these links are themselves connected with facts and events in the State's development that are quite as interesting, and of as far-reaching importance, as those that have been narrated here. Some such suggestion as this, it is hoped, will cross the minds of young students, and lead them to investigate for themselves the interesting intervals that lie between.

It is unfortunately true that there is no history of Georgia in which the dry bones of facts have been clothed with the flesh and blood of popular narrative. Colonel Charles C. Jones saw what was needed, and entered upon the task of writing the

history of the State with characteristic enthusiasm. He had
not proceeded far, however, when the fact dawned upon his
mind that such a work as he contemplated must be for the
most part a labor of love. He felt the influence of cold
neglect from every source that might have been expected to
afford him aid and encouragement. He was almost compelled
to confine himself to a bare recital of facts, for he had reason
to know that, at the end of his task, public inappreciation was
awaiting him.

And yet it seems to the present writer that every person interested in the growth and development of the republic should
turn with eager attention to a narrative embodying the events
that have marked the progress of Georgia. It was in this
State that some of the most surprising and spectacular scenes
of the Revolution took place. In one corner of Georgia those
who were fighting for the independence of the republic made
their last desperate stand ; and if they had surrendered to the
odds that faced them, the battle of King's Mountain would
never have been fought, Greene's southern campaign would
have been crippled, and the struggle for liberty in the south
would have ended in smoke.

It is to illustrate the larger events that these stories have
been written ; and while some of them may seem far away
from this point of view, they all have one common purpose
and tend to one common end.

CONTENTS.

——◦◦——

	PAGE
A SEARCH FOR TREASURE	7
OGLETHORPE AND HIS GENTLE COLONY	20
"THE EMPRESS OF GEORGIA"	28
THE LIBERTY BOYS	41
A GROUP OF CHARACTERS	57
AUNT NANCY HART	69
TWO SOLDIERS OF THE REVOLUTION	84
A WAR OF EXTERMINATION	97
A NEGRO PATRIOT	115
THE YAZOO FRAUD	120
GEORGE MATTHEWS AND JOHN CLARKE	136
AFTER THE REVOLUTION	145
THE COTTON GIN	154
SOME GEORGIA INVENTIONS	163
THE EARLY PROGRESS OF THE STATE	174
THE CREEKS AND THE CREEK WAR	184
TWO FAMOUS INDIAN CHIEFS	199

6

PAGE

REMOVAL OF THE CHEROKEES 216

THE BEGINNING OF PARTIES IN GEORGIA 227

A QUEER CASE 234

GEORGIA WIT AND HUMOR 240

SLAVERY AND SECESSION 251

THE FARMER BOY OF GADDISTOWN 259

GEORGIA IN THE WAR 272

A DARING ADVENTURE 281

THE RECONSTRUCTION PERIOD 297

"THE NEW SOUTH" 307

STORIES OF GEORGIA.

A SEARCH FOR TREASURE.

SO far as written records tell us, Hernando de Soto
and his companions in arms were the first white
men to enter and explore the territory now known on
the map as the State of Georgia. Tradition has small

voice in the matter, but such as it has tells another story. There are hints that other white men ventured into this territory before De Soto and his men beheld it. General Oglethorpe, when he came to Georgia with his gentle colony, which had been tamed and sobered by misfortune and ill luck, was firmly of the opinion that Sir Walter Raleigh, the famous soldier, sailor, and scholar, had been there before him. So believing, the founder of the Georgian Colony carried with him Sir Walter's diary. He was confirmed in his opinion by a tradition, among the Indians of the Yamacraw tribe, that Raleigh had landed where Savannah now stands. There are also traditions in regard to the visits of other white men to Georgia. These traditions may be true, or they may be the results of dreams, but it is certain that De Soto and his picked company of Spaniards were the first to march through the territory that is now Georgia. The De Soto expedition was made up of the flower of Spanish chivalry, — men used to war, and fond of adventure. Some of them were soldiers, anxious to win fame by feats of arms in a new land; some were missionaries, professing an anxiety for the souls of such heathen as they might encounter, but even these men were not unfamiliar with the use of the sword; some were physicians, as ready to kill as to heal; some were botanists, who knew as much about the rapier and the poniard as they did about the stamens, pistils, and petals of the flowers; and some were reporters, men selected to write the history of the expedition. As it turned out, these reporters were entirely faithful to their trust. They told all that happened with a fidelity that leaves nothing to be desired. The record they have left shows that the expedition was bent on finding gold and other treasures.

On the 30th of May, 1539, De Soto's expedition landed at Tampa Bay, Fla., and his men pitched their tents on the beach. The army was not a large one; but it was made up of chosen men, who were used to the dangers of war, and who, as stated before, were fond of adventure. There was but one gray head in the expedition : therefore, though the army was a small one, it was the most enthusiastic and warlike array that had ever been seen in the New World. The soldiers wore rich armor, and the cavalry rode gayly caparisoned horses. The army was accompanied by slaves and mules to bear the burdens. It had artillery and other weapons of war; handcuffs, neck collars, and chains for prisoners; crucibles for refining gold; bloodhounds, greyhounds, and a drove of hogs.

For nearly a year the little army of De Soto wandered about in Florida, ransacking the burying grounds of the Indians in search of treasures, and committing such other depredations as were common to the civilization of that age. When inquiries were made for gold, the Indians always pointed toward the north ; and, following these hints, the expedition pursued its way through Florida, wandering about in the swamps and slashes, but always held together by the enthusiasm of the men and their hopes of securing rich spoils.

On the 3d of March, 1540, De Soto's army left Anhayca, which is said to have been near the site of Tallahassee, and marched northward. Before leaving,

the Spaniards seized from the Indians a large supply of
maize (now commonly known as corn), and appropriated
whatever else struck their fancy. They had spent some
time with the Indians at this town of Anhayca, and had
sent out parties that committed depredations wherever an
Indian settlement could be found. They made slaves of:
many Indians, treating them with more severity than they.
treated their beasts of burden. It is no wonder, therefore,
that the Indians, discovering the greed of the Spaniards
for gold, should have spread rumors that large quantities
of the yellow metal were to be found farther north.

Reports came to the Spaniards of a wonderful Indian
queen who reigned at a place called Yupaha, a settlement as large as a city. One day an Indian boy, who
had been brought to camp with other prisoners, told the
Spaniards a good deal about this great Indian queen.
He said that she ruled not only her own people, but all
the neighboring chiefs, and as far as the Indian settlements extended. The boy told the Spaniards that all
the Indians paid tribute to this great queen, and sent
her fine presents of clothing and gold. De Soto and
his men cared nothing about fine clothing. They were
greedy only for gold and precious stones. They asked
the Indian boy many questions, and he answered them
all. He told how the gold was taken from the earth,
and how it was melted and refined. His description
was so exact that the Spaniards no longer had any doubt.
Their spirits rose mightily, and, after robbing and
plundering the Indians who had fed and sheltered them
during the winter months, they broke up their camp and
moved northward.

Four days after leaving Tallahassee, the Spaniards came to a deep river, which Colonel C. C. Jones, jun., in his "History of Georgia," says was the Ocklockonnee, very close to the southwest boundary of Georgia. Two days later they came to an Indian village from which the inhabitants fled, but a little later a squad of five soldiers was set upon by the Indians hiding near the encampment. One of the Spaniards was killed, while three others were badly wounded. De Soto left this Indian village on the 11th of March, and presently came to a piece of country which the Spanish historian describes as a desert. But it was not a desert then, and it is not a desert now. It was really a pine barren, such as may be seen to this day in what is called the wire-grass region of southern Georgia. In these barrens the soil is sandy and the land level, stretching away for miles. De Soto and his men saw the primeval pines; but these have long since disappeared, and their places are taken by pines of a smaller growth. On the 21st of March, the Spaniards came to the Ocmulgee River, near which they found an Indian town called Toalli.

There will always be a dispute about the route followed by De Soto in his march. This dispute is interesting, but not important. Some say that the expedition moved parallel with the coast until the Savannah River was reached, at a point twenty-five miles below Augusta; but it is just as probable that the route, after reaching the Ocmulgee, was along the banks of that stream and in a northwesterly direction.

At Toalli the Indians had summer and winter houses

to live in, and they had storehouses for their maize. The women wore blankets or shawls made of the fiber of silk grass, and the blankets were dyed vermilion or black. Thenceforward the Indians whom the Spaniards met with were of a higher order of intelligence, and of a more industrious turn, than those left behind in Florida and along the southern boundary of Georgia.

As De Soto marched along, he seized Indians and made guides of them, or made prisoners and held them until he was furnished with guides and interpreters. He also announced to the Indians that he was the Child of the Sun, who had been sent to seek out the greatest Prince and Princess. This made a great impression on the Indians, many of whom were sun worshipers.

Many times during the march the Spaniards were on the point of starvation, and the account of their sufferings as set forth in the history of the expedition is intended to be quite pathetic. We need not pause to shed any tears over these things, for the sufferings the Spaniards endured were nothing compared to the sufferings they inflicted on the Indians. They murdered and robbed right and left, and no doubt the Indians regarded them as demons rather than Christians. More than once when the Spaniards were wandering aimlessly about in the wilderness, they were found by the Indians and saved from starvation. In turn the simple-minded natives were treated with a harshness that would be beyond belief if the sickening details were not piously set forth by the Spanish historian of the expedition.

About the 28th of April the expedition reached the neighborhood of Cutifachiqui, having been told by three Indians whom they had taken, that the queen of that province knew of the approach of the Spaniards, and was awaiting them at her chief town just across the river. As De Soto came to the shore of the stream,

four canoes started from the opposite side. One of them contained a kinswoman of the queen, who had been selected to invite the Spaniards to enter the town. Shortly afterwards the queen came forth from the town, seated on a palanquin or litter, which was borne by the principal men. Coming to the water side, the queen entered a canoe, over the stern of which was stretched an awning to shelter her from the sun.

Under this awning she reclined on cushions; and thus, in company with her chiefs, and attended by many of her people in canoes, she crossed the river to meet De Soto. She landed, and gave the Spaniard a gracious welcome. As an offering of peace and good will, she took from her neck a long string of pearls, and gave the gems to De Soto. She also gave him many shawls and finely dressed deerskins. The Spaniard acknowledged the beautiful gifts by taking from his hand a gold ring set with a ruby, and placing it upon one of the queen's fingers.

The old historian pretends that De Soto and his men were very much impressed by the dignity and courtesy of the Indian queen. She was the first woman ruler they had met in their wanderings. She was tall, finely formed, and had great beauty of countenance. She was both gracious and graceful. All this is set down in the most pompous way by the Spanish chroniclers; but the truth seems to be that De Soto and his men cared nothing for the courtesy and hospitality of the queen, and that they were not moved by her beauty and kindness. The Spaniards crossed the river in canoes furnished by the queen's people, and found themselves surrounded by the most hospitable Indians they had yet seen. They were supplied with everything the land afforded, and rested in comfortable wigwams under the shade of mulberry trees. The soldiers were so delighted with the situation, that they were anxious to form a settlement there; but De Soto refused to forget the only object of the expedition, which was to search for gold and other treasures. His deter-

mination had the desired effect. His men recovered
their energies. While enjoying the hospitality of the
queen, they found out the burial places of her people,
and gathered from the graves, according to the statement of the Spanish historian, "three hundred and fifty
weight of pearls, and figures of babies and birds, made
from iridescent shells."

The mother of the queen lived not far from the town
where the Spaniards were quartered, and, as she was
said to be the owner of many fine pearls, De Soto expressed a desire to see her. Upon hearing this, the
queen sent twelve of her principal men to beg her
mother to come to see the white strangers and the
wonderful animals they had brought with them; but the
mother of the queen was very shrewd. She rebuked
the messengers, and sent them back with some sharp
words for her daughter; and though De Soto did his
best to capture the woman, he was never able to carry
out his purpose.

He then turned his attention to a temple that stood
on the side of a deserted settlement which had formerly
been the chief town of the queen's people. This
temple, as described by the Spanish chronicler, was
more than one hundred steps long by forty broad, the
walls high in proportion, and the roof elevated so as to
allow the water to run off. On the roof were various
shells arranged in artistic order, and the shells were
connected by strings of pearls. These pearls extended
from the top of the roof to the bottom in long festoons,
and the sun shining on them produced a very brilliant
effect. At the door of the temple were twelve giant-

like statues made of wood. These figures were so
ferocious in their appearance, that the Spaniards hesitated for some time before they could persuade themselves to enter the temple.   The statues were armed
with clubs, maces, copper axes, and pikes ornamented
with copper at both ends.   In the middle of the temple
were three rows of chests, placed one upon another
in the form of pyramids.   Each pyramid consisted of
five or six chests, the largest at the bottom, and the
smallest at the top.   These chests, the Spanish chroniclers say, were filled with pearls, the largest containing
the finest pearls, and the smallest only seed pearls.

It is just as well to believe a little of this as to believe
a great deal.   It was an easy matter for the survivors
of the expedition to exaggerate these things, and they
probably took great liberties with the facts; but there
is no doubt that the Indians possessed many pearls.
Mussels like those from which they took the gems are
still to be found in the small streams and creeks of
Georgia, and an enterprising boy might even now be
able to find a seed pearl if he sought for it patiently.

It is not to be doubted that rich stores of pearls were
found.   Some were distributed to the officers and men;
but the bulk of them, strange to say, were left undisturbed, to await the return of the Spaniards another day.
De Soto was still intent on searching for gold, and he
would hear of nothing else.   He would neither settle
among the queen's people for a season, nor return to
Tampa with the great store of pearls discovered.   Being
a resolute man and of few words, he had his way, and
made preparations to journey farther north to the prov·

ince called Chiaha, which was governed by a great Indian king.

The conduct of the Spaniards had been so cruel during their stay at Cutifachiqui, that the queen had come to regard them with fear and hatred, and she refused to supply them with guides and burden bearers. De Soto thereupon placed her under guard; and when he took up his march for Chiaha, the queen who had received him with so much grace, dignity, and hospitality, was compelled to accompany him on foot, escorted by her female attendants. The old Spanish chronicler is moved to remark that "it was not so good usage as she deserved for the good will she shewed and the good entertainment that she had made him." This was the return the Spanish leader made to the queen who had received and entertained his army, — to seize her, place her under guard, and compel her to accompany his expedition on foot.

One reason why De Soto made the queen his prisoner and carried her with the expedition was to use her influence in controlling the Indians along his line of march. The result was all that he could have expected. In all the towns through which the Spaniards passed, the queen commanded the Indians to carry the burdens of the army; and thus they went for a hundred leagues, the Indians obeying the queen without question. After a march of seven days, De Soto arrived at the province of Chelaque, which was the country of the Cherokees. Here the soldiers added to their stores of provisions, and renewed their march; and on May 15 they arrived in the province of Xualla, the chief town of which is supposed to have been situated in the Nacoochee valley. Inclining his course westwardly from the Nacoochee valley, De Soto set out for Gua-xule, which marked the limit of the queen's dominion, and which has been identified as Old Town, in Murray County. On this march the queen made her escape, taking with her a cane box filled with large pearls of great value. This box had been borne by one of the queen's attendants up to the moment when she disappeared from the Spanish camp. De Soto made every effort to recapture the queen. No doubt the bloodhounds, which formed a part of the expedition, were called in to aid in the search; but it was all to no purpose. The queen hid herself as easily as a young partridge hides, and neither men nor dogs could find her. De Soto went on his way, deploring the loss of the valuable pearls.

From Nacoochee to Murray County the march was fatiguing. The route lay over mountains as well as valleys. One of the foot soldiers, Juan Terron (his folly has caused history to preserve his name), grew so weary on this march, that he drew from his wallet a linen bag containing six pounds of pearls. Calling to a cavalryman, Juan Terron offered him the bag of pearls if he would carry them. The cavalryman refused the offer, and told his comrade to keep them. But Juan Terron would not have it so. He untied the bag, whirled it around his head, and scattered the pearls in all directions. This done, he replaced the empty bag in his wallet, and marched on, leaving his companions amazed at his folly. Thirty of the pearls were recovered by the soldiers. The gems were of great size, and perfect in every particular; and it was estimated that the six pounds of pearls would have fetched six thousand ducats in Spain (over twelve thousand dollars). The folly of the foot soldier gave rise to a saying in the army, that is no doubt current in Spain to this day, — "There are no pearls for Juan Terron," which means that a fool makes no profits.

Continuing their march, the Spaniards came to the town of Chiaha, — a site that is now occupied by the flourishing city of Rome. De Soto remained at Chiaha a month, sending out exploring expeditions in search of the much-coveted gold. They found traces of the precious metal, but nothing more. On the 1st of July, 1540, De Soto left Chiaha, going down the valley of the Coosa. His expedition was organized by the spirit of greed. It spread desolation wherever it went, and it ended in disaster and despair. De Soto himself found a grave in the waters of the Mississippi, and the survivors who made their way back home were broken in health and spirits.

An attempt has been made to throw a halo of romance over this march of the Spaniards through the wilderness of the New World, but there is nothing romantic or inspiring about it. It was simply a search for riches, in which hundreds of lives were most cruelly sacrificed, and thousands of homes destroyed.

OGLETHORPE AND HIS GENTLE COLONY.

GENERAL JAMES EDWARD OGLETHORPE, the founder of the Colony of Georgia, was among the few really good and great men that history tells us of. We need to keep a close eye on the antics of history. She places the laurels of fame in the hands of butchers, plunderers, and adventurers, and even assassins share her favors; so that, if we are going to enjoy the feast that history offers us, we must not inquire too closely into the characters of the men whom she makes heroes of. We find, when we come to look into the matter, that but few of those who figured as the great men of the world have been entirely unselfish; and unselfishness is the test of a man who is really good and great. Judged by this test, General Oglethorpe stands among the greatest men known to history.

He had served in the army with distinction, as his father had before him. He was on the staff of the great soldier Eugene of Savoy, and under that commander made himself conspicuous by his fidelity and fearlessness. A story is told of him that is interesting, if not characteristic. While serving under Eugene, he one day found himself sitting at table with a prince of Würtemberg. He was a beardless youngster, and the prince thought to have some sport with him. Taking up a glass of wine, the prince gave it a fillip, so that a little flew in Oglethorpe's face. The young Englishman, looking straight at the prince, and smiling, said, " My prince, that is only a part of the joke as the English know it: I will show you the whole of it." With that he threw a glassful of wine in the prince's face. An old general who sat by laughed dryly, and remarked, " He did well, my prince: you began it."

Born in 1689, Oglethorpe entered the English army when twenty-one years of age. In 1714 he became captain lieutenant of the first troop of the queen's life guards. He shortly afterwards joined Eugene on the continent, and remained with that soldier until the peace of 1718. On the death of his brother, he succeeded to the family estate in England. In 1722 he was elected to Parliament from Haslemere, county of Surrey, and this borough he represented continuously for thirty-two years. His parliamentary career was marked by wise prudence and consistency; and his sympathies were warmly enlisted for the relief of unfortunate soldiers, and in securing reform in the conduct of prisons. In this way Oglethorpe became a philanthropist, and, without intending it, attracted the attention of all England. Pope, the poet, eulogizes his "strong benevolence of soul."

In that day and time, men were imprisoned for debt in England. The law was brutal, and those who executed it were cruel. There was no discrimination between fraud and misfortune. The man who was unable to pay his debts was judged to be as criminal as the man who, though able, refused to pay. Both were thrown into the same prison, and subjected to the same hardships. In "Little Dorrit," Charles Dickens has told something of those unfortunates who were thrown into prison for debt.

There was apparently nothing too atrocious to be sanctioned by the commercial ambition of the English. It armed creditors with the power to impose the most cruel burdens upon their debtors, and it sanctioned the slave trade. Many crimes have been committed to promote the commercial supremacy of Great Britain, and on that blind policy was based the law which suffered innocent debtors to be deprived of their liberty and thrown into prison.

This condition of affairs Oglethorpe set himself to reform; and while thus engaged, he became impressed with the idea that many of the unfortunates, guilty of no crime, and of respectable connections, might benefit themselves, relieve England of the shame of their imprisonment, and confirm and extend the dominion of the mother country in the New World, by being freed from the claims of those to whom they owed money, on condition that they would consent to become colonists in America. To this class were to be added recruits from those who, through lack of work and of means, were likely to be imprisoned on account of their misfortunes. Oglethorpe was also of the opinion that men of means, enterprise, and ambition could be enlisted in the cause; and in this he was not mistaken.

He had no hope whatever of personal gain or private benefit. The plan that he had conceived was entirely for the benefit of the unfortunate, based on broad and high ideas of benevolence; and so thoroughly was this understood, that Oglethorpe had no difficulty whatever in securing the aid of men of wealth and influence. A charter or grant from the government was applied for, in order that the scheme might have the sanction and authority of the government. Accordingly a charter was granted, and the men most prominent in the scheme of benevolence were incorporated under the name of "The Trustees for establishing the Colony of Georgia in America." Georgia in America, was, under the terms of the charter, a pretty large slice of America. It embraced all that part of the continent lying between the Savannah and Altamaha rivers, and extending westerly from the heads of these rivers in direct lines to the South Seas; so that the original territory of Georgia extended from ocean to ocean.

In aid of this enterprise, Oglethorpe not only contributed largely from his private means, and solicited contributions from his wealthy friends, but wrote a tract in which he used arguments that were practical as well as ingenious.

On the 17th of November, 1732, all arrangements having been completed, the "Anne" set sail for the

Colony of Georgia, accompanied by Oglethorpe, who furnished his own cabin, and laid in provisions not only for himself, but for his fellow-passengers. On the 13th of January, 1733, the "Anne" anchored in Charleston harbor. From Charleston the vessel sailed to Port Royal; and the colonists were soon quartered in the barracks of Beaufort-town, which had been prepared for their reception. Oglethorpe left the colonists at Beaufort, and, in company with Colonel William Bull, proceeded to the Savannah River. He went up this stream as far as Yamacraw Bluff, which he selected as the site of the settlement he was about to make. He marked out the town, and named it Savannah. The site was a beautiful one in Oglethorpe's day, and it is still more beautiful now. The little settlement that the founder of the Colony marked out has grown into a flourishing city, and art has added its advantages to those of nature to make Savannah one of the most beautiful cities in the United States.

Close by the site which Oglethorpe chose for his colony was an Indian village occupied by the Yama-craws, — a small tribe, of which Tomochichi was chief. At this point, too, was a trading post, which had been established by a white man named John Musgrove. This man had married a half-breed woman whose Indian name was Coosaponakesee, but who was known as Mary Musgrove. In order to insure the friendly reception of his little colony and its future safety, Oglethorpe went to the village and had a talk with Tomochichi. Mary Musgrove not only acted as interpreter, but used her influence, which was very great, in favor of her husband's countrymen. This was fortunate, for the Indians were very uneasy when they learned that a colony of whites was to be established near their village, and some of them even threatened to use force to prevent it; but Oglethorpe's friendly attitude, and Mary Musgrove's influence, at last persuaded them to give their consent. They made an agreement to cede the necessary land, and promised to receive the colonists in a friendly manner. Oglethorpe returned to Beaufort when he had concluded this treaty, and the Sunday following his return was celebrated as a day of thanksgiving. After religious services there was a barbecue, which, history tells us, consisted of four fat hogs, turkeys, fowls, English beef, a hogshead of punch, a hogshead of beer, and a quantity of wine.

On the 30th of January, 1733, the immigrants set sail from Beaufort, and on the afternoon of the next day they arrived at Yamacraw Bluff. On the site of the town that had already been marked off, they pitched four tents large enough to accommodate all the people. Oglethorpe, after posting his sentinels, slept on the ground under the shelter of the tall pines, near the central watch fire. As a soldier should, he slept soundly. He had planted the new Colony, and thus far all had gone well with him and with those whose interests he had charge of.

To bring these colonists across the ocean, and place them in a position where they might begin life anew, was not a very difficult undertaking; but to plant a colony amongst savages already suspicious of the whites, and to succeed in obtaining their respect, friendship, and aid, was something that required wisdom, courage, prudence, and large experience. This Oglethorpe did; and it is to his credit, that, during the time he had charge of the Colony, he never in any shape or form took advantage of the ignorance of the Indians. His method of dealing with them was very simple. He conciliated them by showing them that the whites could be just, fair, and honorable in their dealings; and thus, in the very beginning, he won the friendship of those whose enmity to the little Colony would have proved ruinous.

Providence favored Oglethorpe in this matter. He had to deal with an Indian chief full of years, wisdom, and experience. This was Tomochichi, who was at the head of the Yamacraws. From this kindly Indian the Georgia Colony received untold benefits. He remained the steadfast friend of the settlers, and used his influence in their behalf in every possible way, and on all occasions. Although he was a very old man, he was strong and active, and of commanding presence. He possessed remarkable intelligence; and this, added

to his experience, made him one of the most remarkable of the Indians whose names have been preserved
in history. There was something of a mystery about
him that adds to the interest which his active friendship
for the whites has given to his name. He belonged
to the tribe of Lower Creeks; but for some reason or
other, he, with a number of his tribemen, had been
banished. The cause of his exile has never been
made known; but at this late day it may be guessed
that he became disgusted with the factional disputes
among the Creeks, and sought in another part of the
territory the peace and repose to which his years of
service had entitled him; and that when he had taken
this step, the factions which he had opposed succeeded
in having him banished. Some such theory as 'this is
necessary to account for the tributes that were paid
to his character and influence by the Creek chiefs who
assembled at Savannah to make a treaty with Oglethorpe. Tomochichi was ninety-one years old when
the Georgia Colony was founded, and he had gathered
about him a number of disaffected Creeks and Yemas-
sees, known as the tribe of the Yamacraws. When
the Creeks came to Savannah to meet Oglethorpe, the
greatest of their chiefs said that he was related to
Tomochichi, who was a good man, and had been a
great warrior.

Thus, with Oglethorpe to direct it, and with Tomochichi as its friend, the little Georgia Colony was
founded, and, as we shall see, thrived and flourished.

"THE EMPRESS OF GEORGIA."

WHEN Oglethorpe landed at Yamacraw Bluff, he was greatly aided in his efforts to conciliate the Indians by the wife of John Musgrove, a half-breed woman whose Indian name was Coosaponakesee. She was known by the colonists as Mary Musgrove, and her friendship for the whites was timely and fortunate. She was Oglethorpe's interpreter in his first interview with Tomochichi. She was very friendly and accommodating, giving aid to Oglethorpe and his colony in every possible way. Finding that she had great influence, and could be made very useful to the colonists, Oglethorpe employed her as interpreter, and paid her yearly one hundred pounds sterling, which in that day was equal to a great deal more than five hundred dollars; but Mary Musgrove earned all that was paid her, and more. She used all her influence in behalf of the whites. She aided in concluding treaties, and also in securing warriors from the Creek nation in the war that occurred between the colonists and the Spaniards who occupied Florida.

General Oglethorpe had a sincere friendship for Mary Musgrove, and his influence over her was such that she never refused a request he made. If Oglethorpe had remained in Georgia, it is probable that the curious episode in which Mary took a leading part would never have occurred.

Oglethorpe left Georgia on the 23d of July, 1743, and never returned. John Musgrove died shortly afterwards, and Mary married a man named Matthews, who also died. She then married a man named Thomas Bosomworth, who had been chaplain to Oglethorpe's regiment. In 1743, before Oglethorpe's departure, Bosomworth had been commissioned to perform all religious and ecclesiastical affairs in Georgia. Previous to that he had accepted a grant of lands, and had taken up his abode in the Colony. He appears to have been a pompous and an ambitious person, with just enough learning to make him dangerous.

Before Mary Musgrove married Bosomworth she had never ceased to labor for the good of the Colony. No sacrifice was too great for her to make in behalf of her white friends. It is true, she had not been fully paid for her services; but she had faith in the good intentions of the government, and was content. In 1744, a year after Oglethorpe's departure from the Colony, Mary married Bosomworth, and after that her conduct was such as to keep the whites in constant fear of massacre and extermination.

In 1745, Thomas Bosomworth went to England and informed the trustees of the Georgia Company that he intended to give up his residence in the Georgia Colony. The next year he returned to Georgia, and violated the regulations of the trustees by introducing six negro slaves on the plantation of his wife near the Altamaha River. This action was at once resented; and President Stephens, who had succeeded Oglethorpe in the management of the Colony's affairs, was ordered to have the negro slaves removed from the territory of Georgia. This was ˙done, and from that time forth Bosomworth and his wife began to plot against the peace and good order of the Georgia Colony. He used the influence of his wife to conciliate the Indians, and secure their sympathy and support. While this was going on, he was busy in preparing a claim against the government of the Colony for the services rendered and losses sustained by his wife, which he valued at five hundred pounds sterling. In her name he also claimed possession of the islands of Ossabaw, St. Catharine, and Sapelo, and of a tract of land near Savannah which in former treaties had been reserved to the Indians.

Bosomworth was shrewd enough not to act alone. In some mysterious way, not clearly told in history, he secured the sympathy and support of Major William Horton, commander of Oglethorpe's regiment stationed at Frederica, and other officers. Colonel Héron, who succeeded Major Horton as commander of the regiment in 1747, was likewise gained over to the cause of the Bosomworths. By the connivance of this officer, a body of Indians, with Malatche at their head, marched to Frederica for a conference. At this conference Malatche made a speech in which he told of the services which his sister Mary had rendered the colonists, and requested that a messenger be sent to England to tell the King that he, Malatche, was emperor of all the Creeks. He declared, also, that Mary, his sister, was confided in by the whole Creek nation, and that the nation had decided to abide by her will and desire.

Bosomworth saw the necessity of pushing the matter forward, and so he suggested to Malatche the importance of having himself crowned as emperor by those who were with him. Accordingly a paper was drawn up giving to Malatche full authority as emperor. This done, Bosomworth was quick to procure from the Creek emperor a deed of conveyance to Thomas and Mary Bosomworth of the islands of Ossabaw, Sapelo, and St. Catharine.

Matters went on peaceably for a while; but Bosomworth was active and energetic, and his wife appears to have been entirely under his control. He bought on credit a great number of cattle from planters in South Carolina, and these he placed on the islands that had been given him by Malatche. When his debts fell due, he was unable to pay them. Rather than surrender the property for which he was unable to pay, he suggested to his wife that she take the title of an independent empress. It is doubtful if she knew what an empress was; but she had an idea, that, if she claimed to be one, she would be able to buy some red calico at the nearest store, as well as an extra bottle of rum. So she fell eagerly into the Rev. Mr. Bosomworth's plans. She sent word to the Creeks that she had suddenly become a genuine empress, and called a meeting of the big men of the nation. The big men assembled; and Mary made a speech, in which she insisted that she was the Empress of Georgia. She must have been a pretty good talker; for the Indians

became very much excited, and pledged themselves to
stand by her to the last drop of their blood.

Having thus obtained the support of the Indians,
Mary set out for Savannah, accompanied by a large
body of them. She sent before her a messenger to

inform the president of the Province that she had become empress over the whole territory belonging to the
Upper and Lower Creeks; that she was on her way to
demand the instant surrender of all the lands that had

belonged to both nations; and that, if there should be
any serious opposition to her demands, the settlement
would be attacked and destroyed.

It was a dark hour for the colonists, who were vastly
outnumbered by the Indians. The president and council were disturbed by the bold threats made by Mary
Bosomworth. Their first plan was to meet the Indians
peaceably, and, by gentle measures, find an opportunity to seize Mary Bosomworth and ship her to England. In the town of Savannah there were only one
hundred and seventy men able to bear arms. The
president of the Province sent a messenger to Mary,
while she and her followers were still several miles
distant, warning her to give up her wild scheme.
Mary sent back a message expressing her contempt
for the Colony and its officials. Thereupon the president of the Province determined to put the best possible
face on the matter, and receive Mary and her savage
followers boldly. Accordingly the militia was ordered
under arms; and as the Indians entered the town, they
were stopped by Colonel Noble Jones, who, at the head
of a company of horse, demanded to know whether
they came with friendly or hostile intentions. He received no satisfactory answer to his demand, where-
upon he informed the Indians that they must ground
their arms, as he had orders not to permit an armed
man among them to set foot within the town. The
Indians submitted to the unexpected demand, but with
great reluctance.

Having grounded their arms, the Indians were allowed to enter the town. They marched in regular

order, headed by Thomas Bosomworth, who, decked out in full canonical robes, with Mary by his side, was followed by the various chiefs according to their rank. The army of Indians made a formidable appearance as they marched into the town, and the inhabitants were terror-stricken at the sight. They marched to the parade ground, where they found the militia drawn up to receive them. Here they were saluted with fifteen guns, and then conducted to the president's house. When the Indians were assembled there, Thomas and Mary Bosomworth were ordered to withdraw. Then the president and council asked the Indian chiefs in a friendly manner why they visited the town in so large a body, not having been sent for by any person in lawful authority. The Indians replied that Mary, their empress, was to speak for them, and that they would abide by what she said. They had heard that she was to be made a prisoner and sent across the great waters, and they wanted to know why they were to lose their queen. They said they intended no harm to the whites, and begged that their arms might be restored to them. Then, after talking with Bosomworth and his wife, they would return and settle all public affairs. Their arms were restored to them, but orders were given that on no account should any ammunition be issued until the true purpose of their visit was made known.

The Indians then had a conference with Mary Bosomworth, and on the following day began to conduct themselves riotously, running up and down the streets like madmen. As all the men were obliged to perform guard duty, the women were compelled to remain alone in their houses. They were in a constant state of terror and alarm, expecting every moment to be set upon and killed by the unruly savages. While the confusion was at its worst, a rumor was circulated that the Indians had cut off the head of the president of the council. The report was false; but the colonists were in such a state of excitement, that they could scarcely be restrained from firing on the Indians. The situation was very critical. Great prudence was necessary in order to prevent bloodshed, and save the town from destruction.

At this crisis orders were given to the militia to lay hold of Thomas Bosomworth, and place him in close confinement. When this order was carried out, Mary became frantic, and made threats of vengeance against the whole Colony. She cursed General Oglethorpe, declared that his treaties were fraudulent, and ordered the colonists to depart from her territory. She raved furiously, and claimed control over the entire earth. But while engaged in cutting up these extraordinary capers, she kept an eye on the leading men among the Indians, who she knew could be easily bribed.

The president of the Province, finding that nothing could be done with the Indians while they remained under the influence of their so-called empress, caused Mary to be privately arrested, and placed her under guard with her husband. When this was done, quiet was at once restored. The Indians ceased to be boisterous. When the time seemed to be ripe, the president of the Province employed men acquainted with the Creek language to entertain the chiefs and their warriors in the friendliest way. A feast was prepared; and in the midst of it the chiefs were told that Bosomworth had become involved in debt, and was anxious to secure not only all the lands of the Creeks, but also a large share of the bounty paid to them by the King of England, so that he might be able to pay his creditors in Carolina. He was also told that the King's presents were intended only for the Indians; that the lands near the town were reserved for them for their encampments; that the sea islands were reserved for them to hunt upon when they should come to bathe in the salt waters; and that neither Mary nor her husband had any right to these lands, which were the common property of the Creek nations.

For the moment this policy was successful. Even Malatche, Mary's brother, seemed to be satisfied; and many of the chiefs declared that they were convinced that Bosomworth had deceived them, and that they would trust him no more. But Malatche, at his own request, had another talk with Thomas and Mary Bosomworth, and was again won over to support their wild pretensions; so that, when the Indians were gathered together to receive their shares of the royal bounty, Malatche stood up in the midst of them, and delivered a most violent speech in favor of the claims of Mary as the Empress of Georgia. He declared that she had three thousand warriors at her command, and that every man of them would take up arms in her defense. At the conclusion of his speech, Malatche drew forth a paper and presented it to the president of the council. This paper was merely the sum and substance of Malatche's speech; and it was so clearly the production of Bosomworth, that the effect was far different from what the Indians had expected. The astonishment of the president and council was so apparent, that Malatche begged to have the paper again, so that he might deliver it to the person from whom he had received it.

It was important that another conference should be had with the Indians. Accordingly they were called together again; and the president of the Province made an address, recalling to their minds the fact that when General Oglethorpe and his colony landed in Georgia, they found Mary, then the wife of John Musgrove, living in a hut at Yamacraw; that at that time she was comparatively poor and friendless, being neglected and despised by the Creeks, and going about in rags; that General Oglethorpe, finding that she could speak both the English and the Creek tongues, employed her as an interpreter, gave her rich clothes, and made her a woman of some consequence; that she was respected by the colonists until she married Thomas Bosomworth, but from that time forth they no longer had any confidence in her; that she had no lands of her own; and that General Oglethorpe had no treaty with her, but dealt with the old and wise leaders of the Creeks, who voluntarily surrendered their waste lands to the whites. The president then went on to show that Mary's claims had been invented by Thomas Bosomworth as an easy means of paying a debt of four hundred pounds which he owed in South Carolina for cattle, and that his quarrel with the colonists was due to the fact that they had refused to give him a third part of the royal bounty which belonged by right to the Indians.

At this point the Creek chiefs begged the president to stop. They had heard enough to convince them, they said, and now they wanted to smoke the pipe of peace. Apparently this was a happy ending to a very serious dispute. But at the very moment when everything was serene, Mary Bosomworth made her appearance amongst those who were patching up their differences. She had escaped from her guards, and, having secured a supply of rum, now made her appearance drunk and furious. She filled the air with threats. The president told her, that, unless she ceased her efforts to poison the minds of the Indians, he would again order her into close confinement. Thereupon Mary turned to Malatche and told him what the president had said. In a rage, Malatche seized his arms, and, calling to the rest of the Indians to do the same, dared the whites to touch the empress. The uproar was great. Every Indian had his tomahawk in his hand, and the council expected nothing less than instant death.

At this moment, Captain Noble Jones, who commanded the guard, ordered the Indians to deliver up their arms. The savages were overawed by the coolness and courage of this intrepid officer. They yielded up their arms, and Mary was shut in a private room, and a guard set over her. There she was securely kept, and while the Indians remained she had no further communication with them. Her husband was then sent for, and the president and council tried to reason with him; but he remained obstinate, declaring that he would stand up for his wife's rights to the last. Finding Bosomworth unreasonable, the council caused him to be seized and confined. This done, the authorities then set about persuading the Indians to leave the town peaceably and return to their own settlements. This the savages did after a while, leaving Savannah in small parties until all were gone.

Finding himself no longer supported by the Indians, Thomas Bosomworth at last repented of his folly. He wrote to the president and council, apologizing for his wanton conduct. He acknowledged the title of his wife to be groundless, and relinquished all claim to the lands of the Province. Though his offense had been serious, the colonists pardoned him, and thus ended the career of Coosaponakesee as Empress of Georgia.

And yet, after all, the Rev. Thomas Bosomworth had his way. Mary seems to have lived long; and her husband pressed her claims in London, so that, when Henry Ellis was made governor of the Province, he was authorized, in 1759, to sell the islands of Ossabaw and Sapelo, as well as other Indian lands near Savannah, and out of the moneys received to settle the demands of the Bosomworths, and to give them a title to the Island of St. Catharine, which they had settled and improved. Mary Bosomworth was given four hundred and fifty pounds for goods she had expended in the King's service, and it was provided also that she should be allowed sixteen hundred and fifty pounds for her services as agent. In addition, she was given two thousand pounds, the sum for which Ossabaw and Sapelo sold at auction. A grant of St. Catharine Island was also made to Mary Bosomworth; so that it may be considered that she was richly rewarded for the many good turns she did the colonists in her better days, before her mind had been poisoned by the Rev. Mr. Bosomworth.

I N 1765, what is
known as the
Stamp Act was passed
by the Parliament of
Great Britain, in spite
of all the protests made by the agents of the Colonies.
The people of the Colonies felt that taxation without
representation was an exercise of power not to be
tolerated.

The Stamp Act itself was a very small matter; but
many of the American Colonies had been setting up
claims of independence in various matters. As Benjamin Franklin said, the British nation was provoked by
these claims of independence, and all parties proposed
by this piece of legislation to settle the question once for

all. While the agents of the Colonies, and among them Franklin, protested against the Stamp Act, none of them supposed that it would be met by armed resistance; and yet the terms of the act were insolent and sweeping. It was provided that if the stamps were not used, "marriages would be null and void, notes of hand valueless, ships at sea prizes to the first captors, suits at law impossible, transfers of real estate invalid, inheritances irreclaimable." In spite of these sweeping terms, Benjamin Franklin did not doubt that the act would be carried into effect, and other patriotic Americans thought that the colonists should submit. Even James Otis of Boston, who was afterwards among the first to advocate the calling of an American congress to deliberate upon the propriety of the acts of Great Britain, was of this opinion.

The Georgia authorities regarded the stamp duty as just as any that could be generally imposed on the Colonies, though the manner of imposing it greatly inspired alarm. But while the other Colonies were hesitating, a voice was heard in Virginia. Patrick Henry, speaking for the Virginians, made an eloquent protest against the law, and his boldness kindled into flames the spirit of opposition that had been smoldering in all the Colonies. The Sons of Liberty were organized North and South. In Georgia they were known as "Liberty Boys." "Liberty, property, and no stamps!" was the cry, and it was a cry that stirred the country from one end to the other.

The congress suggested by James Otis of Boston assembled on Monday, the 7th of October, 1765.

Georgia had no delegates in the congress, but was represented by a messenger who was sent to obtain a copy of the proceedings. Such representation was not because the Colony of Georgia failed to sympathize with the purpose for which the congress was called, but was entirely due to the influence and popularity of Governor Wright, the royal governor, who was not only a good man personally, but wise, prudent, and far-seeing. Owing to his exertions, Georgia was not represented in the person of delegates. The speaker of the Georgia House of Assembly had indeed called a convention of the members for the purpose of selecting delegates to the Colonial Congress called to meet in New York, and sixteen members had responded to the call; but such was the influence of Governor Wright, that these members of the assembly were prevailed upon not to send delegates to the congress. But they could not be prevented from preparing and sending a response to the Massachusetts invitation. They had resolved, they said, to support heartily every measure that might be suggested for the support of the common rights of the Colonies.

We learn from the letters of Governor Wright, written to the Earl of Halifax, that it was as much as he could do (and he was a very active as well as a very wise governor) to prevail on the people to maintain at least the outward show of loyalty to the King. And he was not successful even in this, for he informs another correspondent (Mr. Secretary Conway) on the 31st of January, 1766, that the same spirit of "sedition, or rather rebellion, which first appeared at Bos-

ton," had reached Georgia, and that he had been constantly engaged for the space of three months in trying
to convince the people that they ought to submit to the
King's authority until they could point out their grievances and apply for redress in a constitutional way.
Governor Wright also states to the same correspondent
that he has had much trouble in preserving from destruction at the hands of the people the stamp papers
that had been forwarded for the collection of the tax.
He received "incendiary" letters; he had to issue proclamations against riots and "tumultuous and unlawful
assemblies;" and he had also to take measures against
the Liberty Boys, who began to have private meetings,
and who had formed themselves into a society to oppose
and prevent the distribution of the stamp papers.

In short, the good governor was kept in a constant
state of alarm lest the Liberty Boys should seize some
advantage and cause his Majesty the King of England
to have a moment of grief. The Liberty Boys were so
active, and made so many threatening demonstrations,
that Governor Wright was driven to what he describes
as extreme measures. He was compelled to send the
obnoxious stamp papers to a place of safety to prevent
the people from destroying them; and when he had the
papers securely hidden, he was compelled to place men
on duty day and night to protect the precious stamps.
He was obliged to send a posse of men to protect the
stamp distributer by hiding him, and was then moved to
send him into the country for a season, in order to avoid
the resentment of the people; and then, after all his
trouble, the good governor found that the people had

determined not to apply for any papers, stamped or un-stamped, until the King had acted on the petitions sent from the Colonies. No wonder that he was moved to call it "a wretched situation." It was indeed a wretched situation for one who had no higher ideas of duty than to continue to serve the King and oppose the interests of the people.

There was something more of an uproar in South Carolina than in Georgia ; but the truth of history appears to be that the resistance offered to the Stamp Act in Georgia was much more serious than that displayed in Carolina. Although Governor Wright used all his influence to support the act, the people exercised so much vigilance in watching the stamp papers and the officer sent to issue them, that none of the papers found their way into use.

The Colonies were bordering on a state of revolution, when, through the influence of the Earl of Chatham, the Stamp Act was repealed. There was great rejoicing among the people, and a general manifestation of a renewal of loyalty to the mother country. But the seeds of dissension had been sown. The Stamp Act, unnecessary and uncalled for, had given the people cause to ponder over their real relations to the Crown ; and out of the discussion that had taken place arose a spirit of independence that grew and thrived and spread day by day.

In short, the repeal of the Stamp Act gave the people of the Colonies only momentary satisfaction. Their success in securing its repeal gave them a new taste for liberty of action, and a new sense of their importance as individuals. But King George III. was never satisfied with the repeal of the Stamp Act of 1765. He declared that it had wounded the Majesty of England. It fretted him, and the irritation that he felt extended like a contagion to his cabinet. When the Earl of Chatham died, there was no statesman to take his place. The mantle of his office fell on Charles Townshend, who was more anxious to please the King than to secure good government to the people of the Colonies. He was anxious for the British Government to assert with vigor its right to govern the Colonies as it saw fit.

Meanwhile the spirit of independence in the Colonies continued to assert itself more openly day by day, and the determination grew among them not to submit to taxation without representation in Parliament. The organization of Sons of Liberty and Liberty Boys grew and spread both North and South. One of the most fruitful causes of discontent was the fact that Georgia and the other Colonies were compelled to depend upon the will of the British Government in all matters. Every act passed by a colonial assembly must receive the sanction of the British Parliament before it became a law. Petitions were disregarded. Frequently there was a delay of two years between the passage of an act by the Colonial General Assembly and its ratification. But every measure had to receive the approval of the Crown. While the affairs of the country were in this peculiar condition, the people became more and more dissatisfied.

It is now known that Governor James Wright, loyal to the King as he proved himself to be, was fully sensible of the injustice to which the Colonies were compelled to submit. On the 15th of August, 1769, he addressed a letter to the Earl of Hillsborough, which was not read until fifteen months after it was written. In this letter the governor warned the British cabinet that the Colonies would never submit to taxation without representation. There was no disaffection, he said, toward the King or the royal family, but simply a determination on the part of the people to stand on their rights. But the governor's letter lay unread for fifteen months, and there was no reply to the numerous petitions sent from the Colonies. At last the Americans determined to appeal to the pockets instead of to the sentiments of the people of Great Britain. They determined to import no goods whatever that could be manufactured or produced at home.

This determination, instead of causing the British people to conciliate the Americans by securing the repeal of unfriendly laws, turned the popular opinion against the Colonies; and this feeling was intensified by the Boston Tea Party. A bill was passed by both Houses of the British Parliament to close the port of Boston, and the discussion of the measure gave an opportunity to some of the statesmen of the mother country to show their spite. Another law was passed, limiting and cutting down the power of the representative assembly of Massachusetts, and providing that town meetings should not be held except on permission in writing from the royal governor. Another act was passed, giving the governor of the Province the power to send to Great Britain or to other Colonies persons indicted for murder or charged with capital crimes committed in aiding the government of Massachusetts. These acts, intended to humiliate the Colonies, had the effect of inflaming them, and the Liberty Boys grew in numbers and determination.

On the 20th of July, 1774, "The Georgia Gazette," published at Savannah, contained an invitation to the

people of the Province to meet at Tondee's Tavern on the 27th of July to take into consideration the unjust laws that had been passed by the British Parliament. The cause of Massachusetts was the cause of all. The meeting was held, and stood adjourned to the 10th of August, in order to give all the parishes an opportunity to be represented by delegates. Governor Wright, loyal to the last, issued a proclamation warning the people of the Province to avoid attending the meeting; but the proclamation was disregarded, and a meeting of the people of the Province was held at Tondee's Tavern on the 10th of August, 1774. Resolutions were adopted, declaring that his Majesty's subjects in America owed the same allegiance, and were entitled to the same rights and privileges, as their fellow-subjects in Great Britain; that the act lately passed for blockading the port of Boston was contrary to the British constitution; that the act for abolishing the charter of Massachusetts Bay tended to the subversion of American rights; that the Parliament of Great Britain had not, nor ever had, the right to tax his Majesty's American subjects; and that every demand for the support of government should be by requisition made to the several houses of representatives.   The resolutions covered all the grievances of the people of the Colonies.

Meanwhile, Governor Wright was not idle.   He called a convention of Royalists, which met, and signed a protest against the resolutions.   Copies of this protest were made, and sent into all the parishes, by the governor's friends.   Under pressure, many timid men who were really in sympathy with the Liberty Boys signed the protest.   The signatures of dead men were used, and other frauds practiced, in order to make the demonstration in favor of the King sufficient to overawe those who had pledged themselves to American independence.   In all this, Governor Wright was aided by the fact that the only newspaper in the Province, "The Georgia Gazette," was under his control.   He was also aided by the geographical situation of Georgia, and by his own personal popularity.   He had made a good governor.   He had worked as hard for the prosperity and progress of the Province as he now worked to prevent the people from joining the movement for independence.

The governor was successful to the extent that he

was able to prevent Georgia from sending duly accredited representatives to the First Continental Congress; and this fact has been taken by some writers of history to mean that the spirit of liberty and independence was not as earnest and as enthusiastic in Georgia as in the other Provinces. Later, when Georgia was overrun by British and Tory influences, and appeared to be conquered, ill-natured critics recalled the fact that her people were slow to join hands with those who advocated resistance to tyranny.

When the South Carolina delegates to the First Continental Congress returned to their homes, bearing with them copies of the Declaration of Colonial Rights, the Liberty Boys of Georgia renewed their movement with great zeal. Copies of the Declaration were distributed throughout the Province. The result was, that the Liberty Boys grew steadily stronger in numbers, and more defiant in action. An idea of the situation at this time may be gathered from a letter written by Governor Wright to the Earl of Dartmouth on the 13th of December, 1774. He declared that the spirit of independence, or, as he called it, the spirit of enthusiasm, which many were possessed of before, "is raised to such a height of frenzy, that God knows what the consequences may be, or what man or whose property may escape their resentment."

No doubt the amiable governor misunderstood the situation. What he regarded as "frenzy" was merely the eager desire and the determination of the Liberty Boys of Georgia to redeem themselves in the eyes of their brethren in the other Colonies. They were humiliated by their failure to send representatives to the Continental Congress, and they endeavored to redeem themselves by increased zeal and enthusiasm.

They arranged to hold a provincial congress in Savannah on the 18th of January, 1775. Governor Wright, on hearing of this, determined to convene the Provincial General Assembly on the same day, hoping and believing that this would prevent a meeting of the Provincial Congress, or greatly hamper its action. But the governor was mistaken. The General Assembly met in response to the call, and so did the Provincial Congress. Governor Wright addressed the members, declaring to them the danger of the situation, and imploring them to be prudent and loyal. The upper house of the General Assembly made a response agreeable to the governor's expectations, but the lower house gave to its address a tone of independence that was not at all pleasing to the King's officer. He showed his displeasure, and placed a serious obstacle in the way of the Liberty Boys by adjourning the General Assembly until the 9th of the following May. The Assembly had met on the 18th of January, and was adjourned on the 10th of February; so that the Liberty Boys, who made up a majority of the lower house, had no time to appoint delegates to the Philadelphia congress soon to be held, nor to take any official action in behalf of the independence of Georgia.

Governor Wright's plans were certainly very shrewdly laid. His adjournment of the General Assembly not only hampered the Provincial Congress (or convention) that had met at Savannah simultaneously with the legislature, but threw the delegates into confusion and disorder, and was the means of causing the convention to adjourn without taking such action as the friends of liberty hoped for. All that it did was to elect three representatives to the Philadelphia congress. This was something, but it was not enough. The Liberty Boys expected the Provincial Convention to adopt all the measures and resolutions suggested by the Continental Congress. They therefore felt mortified when the convention adjourned, and left Georgia still outside the continental association.

This event was a serious embarrassment to the other Colonies, and aroused the anger of those friends of liberty who were unable to understand the peculiar conditions that surrounded the movement for independence in Georgia. The friends of liberty in South Carolina were so indignant, that they denounced the Georgians "as unworthy the rights of freemen, and as inimical to the liberties of their country." Throughout the Colonies, the partisans of American independence were deeply wounded by the apparent hesitation of the Georgians, while the Royalists were delighted.

Though the Provincial Convention remained in session only seven days before adjourning, the delegates of St. John's Parish had withdrawn from the body. These delegates insisted on an emphatic indorsement of the acts of the Continental Congress, and they retired as soon as they found there would be some difficulty in bringing some of the hesitating members to their way of thinking. They retired, and selected Dr. Lyman Hall to represent St. John's in the Philadelphia congress. He took his seat in that body, and although he cast no vote, he made his voice heard in the discussions.

In spite of all the drawbacks which the Liberty Boys in Georgia had experienced, their enthusiasm did not cool. They never ceased their efforts, and the independence movement continued to grow. The public mind became more and more inflamed with resentment against the tyranny of King George and his Parliament, as the people heard of the progress of events in the more northern Colonies. By the 10th of May the people of Savannah had heard of the shedding of American blood by British troops at Lexington and Concord. As the news spread from parish to parish, the people became aroused, and the response of public sentiment was all that American patriots could expect.

The first response of the Liberty Boys at Savannah was to seize the ammunition stored in the magazine. This event occurred on the night of the 11th of May, and was planned and carried out by the members of the Council of Safety. About six hundred pounds of powder fell into the hands of the Liberty Boys. Some was sent to South Carolina, and the rest was hidden in the garrets and cellars of the patriots who had seized it. Tradition says that some of this powder was sent to Massachusetts, where it was used by the patriots who drove the British before them at the battle of Bunker Hill.

Other events occurred that showed the temper of the Liberty Boys. On the 4th of June, when Governor Wright came to fire salutes in honor of King George's birthday, he found the cannon had been spiked, dismounted, and rolled to the bottom of the bluff. On the 5th of June the first liberty pole in the Colony was set up at Savannah. A young man named Hopkins, who spoke contemptuously of the members of the Committee of Public Safety was seized by a mob, tarred and feathered, placed in an illuminated cart, and paraded up and down the streets of Savannah.

As the days went by, the independence movement in Georgia became more enthusiastic, the Liberty Boys more active. The first vessel armed and equipped for naval warfare during the Revolution was fitted up by the Liberty Boys of Georgia under the authority of the Provincial Convention, which had assembled in Savannah on the 4th of July, 1775. This event is interesting. The Carolina Committee of Safety had heard that a British ship had sailed for Georgia with a cargo of powder intended for the Indians and for the use of the Royalists. The Carolinians at once resolved to capture the ship and seize the cargo. To that end, two barges, manned by forty well-armed men, were embarked from Beaufort, and went to the mouth of the Savannah River, where they encamped on a point that commanded a full view of Tybee Lighthouse. The Provincial Convention, hearing of this expedition, offered to assist the officers in every way possible. There was an armed British schooner in the river at that time; and the Liberty Boys of Savannah determined to join forces with the Carolinians at Tybee, and effect her capture. For this purpose a schooner was equipped by the Provincial Convention, and placed under command of Captain Bowen and Joseph Habersham. This vessel was armed with ten carriage guns and swivels, and carried fifty men. The British armed vessel was not inclined to enter into a contest, but, when the Georgia schooner appeared, weighed anchor and sailed away. The schooner then took position beyond the harbor bar, and waited for the ship carrying the cargo of powder. She had not long to wait. On the 10th of July, 1775, the powder ship, commanded by Captain Maitland, made her appearance. Before entering Tybee Inlet, however, Captain Maitland saw the armed schooner. Suspecting that he was about to fall into a trap, he brought his vessel round, tacked, and stood out to sea. But he had gone too far. The Georgia schooner gave chase, and soon overtook and captured the ship. It was a fortunate capture for the Colonies. Five thousand pounds of powder were sent to Philadelphia, and nine thousand fell to the share of Georgia.

The convention that commissioned the first armed

vessel of the Revolution did more important work than this. It placed the Province of Georgia in political union with her sister Colonies, and gave her fellowship with those struggling Provinces. She was welcomed into the United Colonies with joyful demonstrations by the Continental Congress. By the 15th of April, 1776, the Liberty Boys in Georgia were so strong that Governor Wright had taken refuge on one of the King's vessels at Tybee; and on that date the patriots took full charge of the government of the Province. Archibald Bulloch was the first republican president of Georgia.

This is how the Liberty Boys took the Province of Georgia from his Majesty the King, and made a free and independent government. Their struggle did not end here, but the details of that struggle must be left to history to relate.

A GROUP OF CHARACTERS.

THE Revolutionary War in Georgia developed some very romantic figures, which are known to us rather by tradition than by recorded history. First among them, on the side of the patriots, was Robert Sallette. Neither history nor tradition gives us the place of his birth or the date of his death; yet it is known that he played a more important part in the struggle in the Colony than any man who had no troops at his command. He seems to have slipped mysteriously on the scene at the beginning of the war. He fought bravely, even fiercely, to the end, and then, having nothing else to do, slipped away as mysteriously as he came. "In Liberty County," says history, "there lived during the Revolution a man by the name of Robert Sallette, distinguished for his opposition to the Tories. It is not known with certainty to what particular command he was attached. He appears to have been a sort of roving character, doing things in his own way." Here is the mystery of romance to begin with. Here is the wanderer, — the character so dear to the imagination of youth.

"The Tories," says history further, "stood very much in dread of him; and well they might, for never had they a more formidable foe." Here, then, is the hero and the wanderer combined in one person, and that person fighting for the holiest cause in which man can take up arms, — the rights and liberties of the people. What more could be asked?

Curious as we may be to know something of the personal history of Robert Sallette, it is not to be found chronicled in the books. The French twist to his name makes it probable that he was a descendant of those unfortunate Acadians who, years before, had been stripped of their lands and possessions in Nova Scotia by the British, their houses and barns burned, and they themselves transported away from their homes. They were scattered at various points along the American coast. Some were landed at Philadelphia, and some were carried to Louisiana. Four hundred were sent to Georgia. The British had many acts of cruelty to answer for in those days, but none more infamous than this treatment of the gentle and helpless Acadians. It stands in history to-day a stain upon the British name.

Another fact that leads to the belief that Robert Sallette was a descendant of the unfortunate Acadians was the ferocity with which he pursued the British and the Tories. The little that is told about him makes it certain that he never gave quarter to the enemies of his country.

His name was a terror to the Tories. One of them, a man of considerable means, offered a reward of one hundred guineas to any person who would bring him the head of Robert Sallette. The Tory had never seen Sallette, but his alarm was such that he offered a reward large enough to tempt some one to assassinate the daring partisan. When Sallette heard of the reward, he disguised himself as a farmer, and provided himself with a pumpkin, which he placed in a bag. With the bag swinging across his shoulder, he made his way to the house of the Tory. He was invited in, and deposited the bag on the floor beside him, the pumpkin striking the boards with a thump.

"I have brought you the head of Robert Sallette," said he. "I hear that you have offered a reward of one hundred guineas for it."

"Where is it?" asked the Tory.

"I have it with me," replied Sallette, shaking the loose end of the bag. "Count me out the money and take the head."

The Tory, neither doubting nor suspecting, counted out the money, and placed it on the table.

"Now show me the head," said he.

Sallette removed his hat, tapped himself on the forehead, and said, "Here is the head of Robert Sallette!"

The Tory was so frightened that he jumped from the room, and Sallette pocketed the money and departed.

On one occasion Robert Sallette is known to have spared the lives of two Tories, at least for a little while. Once when he and Andrew Walthour (for whom Walthourville in Georgia is named) and another man were riding along a narrow trail late in the afternoon, they met three other riders whom they suspected to be Tories. The plan that Sallette and his companions adopted to capture the men was very simple. Andrew Walthour, who was riding in front, was to pass the first and second men, Robert Sallette to pass the first. As Walthour came to the third man when Sallette had come to the second, and their companion to the first, the Liberty Boys seized the guns of the three simultaneously. The men had no opportunity either to fight or escape.

"Dismount, gentlemen!" said Sallette. Then he addressed himself to the leader. "What is your name?"

In reply to this, a fictitious name was given, as Sallette and his companions afterwards found out.

"Where is your camp?" asked Sallette.

"We are from over the river," answered the man, meaning the Altamaha.

"Where did you cross?"

"At Beards Ferry." This was where the Whigs and the Liberty Boys were most numerous.

"That is not true!" exclaimed Sallette.

Then he turned to the second man, asked the same questions, and received the same replies. He turned to the third man, asked the same questions, and received the same replies.

"If you do not tell me the truth," exclaimed Sallette to this last man, "I'll cut off your head!"

The man persisted, and Sallette was as good as his word. The others begged for their lives, and declared that they would guide Sallette straight to their camp. This they did; and Sallette, aided by his prisoners, captured a large party of Tories.

Once when Robert Sallette and Andrew Walthour were marching with the advance guard of the American troops, they suddenly met the advance guard of the British. A short but sharp skirmish followed, during which a very large man of the British guard was killed. Observing that the dead man wore a pair of good boots, Sallette determined to get them. While he was pulling them off in the midst of a furious fire from the enemy, his companions called out to him to come away or he would surely be killed. "I must have the boots!" cried Sallette to his companions. "I want them for little John Way!"

Here was fun in the midst of tragedy; for it is said that little John Way could have put both his feet and his fists into one of the boots.

One day Sallette dressed himself up as a British officer and accepted an invitation to dine with a party of the enemy. Suddenly, in the midst of the toasting and drinking, Sallette drew his sword, killed the men who sat to the right and left of him, sprang on his horse, and rode off unhurt, though he was in such a hurry that he had no time to throw the bridle reins over the horse's head.

At the White House, near Sunbury, Major Baker, of the patriot army, with thirty men, attacked and defeated a party of Tories under command of Captain Goldsmith.

Among the slain was Lieutenant Gray, whose head was almost severed from his body by a stroke of Robert Sallette's sword.

On many occasions, when a battle was in progress, Sallette would detach himself from the American army, gain the rear of the enemy, and kill many men before he was discovered. If this brave man was indeed a descendant of the Acadians, he avenged the wrongs of many of his countrymen.

Another character who attracted attention during the War of the Revolution was Patrick Carr, whose hatred of the Tories made his name celebrated among the Liberty Boys of Georgia. Paddy Carr, as he was called, lived and died in Jefferson County. He was born in Ireland, but came to Georgia before the Revolution. When the independence movement began, he threw himself into it with all the ardor of his race. Owing to the cruelty of the Tories, he conceived a special hatred against them. He showed them no quarter. History gives but a word or two to his achievements, but tradition still keeps his name alive in the region where he operated. Like Sallette, he was an independent partisan; but, unlike Sallette, his operations were among those who could remember well enough, but who would not take the trouble to preserve the particulars of even the least of his exploits. We know that Patrick Carr lived. We know that he became famous where recklessness and daring were common. But that is nearly all we know. It is said of him that during the war he killed one hundred Tories with his own hands. Once, when praised for his bravery, he smiled and shook his head, saying that he would have made a very good soldier, but the Lord had given him a heart that was too merciful. He no doubt remembered the atrocities of the Tories in the section that is now Jefferson, Columbia, Burke, and Wilkes counties. The cruelties they committed in that region during the Revolution have no parallel in civilized warfare.

Among the adventurous characters of that time, on the side of the British, Daniel McGirth stands easily first. The history of his career during the war is a strange one. He was born in South Carolina, and entered into the struggle against the British with the utmost enthusiasm. He was a brave man, a hard fighter, and one of the most active of those who took up arms against the King. He was an expert woodsman, and was at home in the saddle. He was assigned to duty as a scout, and was better equipped for that service, perhaps, than any man in the American army. The ease with which he secured information of the enemy's movements and plans, and the energy that marked his movements, made his services of great value to the patriot cause. This was not thoroughly appreciated by some of the officers under whom McGirth acted.

He brought with him into the army a mare which he called "The Gray Goose." She is said to have been an elegant animal, and McGirth was very proud of her. With this mare under him, he always felt safe from pursuit. One of the American officers, who was a good judge of horseflesh, and who probably wanted to "cut a dash," as the saying is, saw this beautiful mare, and coveted her. Finding that McGirth scorned all offers to sell her, the officer adopted various means to obtain her. These efforts were resisted by McGirth, mainly on the ground that the mare was his own private property, and that she was essential to the duties he was called on to perform. Failing to gain his ends in this way, the officer continued to worry McGirth in other ways. He no doubt did something to rouse the ire of the scout, who was an irritable man, and who felt the importance of the service he was rendering to the cause. It is not now known how McGirth insulted the officer, — whether in a moment of passion he struck him, or whether he merely used rough language to him.

Whatever the offense, McGirth was placed under arrest, tried by a court-martial, found guilty of violating the articles of war, and sentenced to be whipped. He received this punishment, and was placed in confinement again, where he was to remain until he received another whipping. While thus held, he saw his mare picketed near the camp, and he immediately resolved to escape. He was successful in this. Once free, he secured The Gray Goose, leaped into the saddle, turned around, and, in the face of his pursuers, pronounced threats of vengeance against all the Americans for his ill treatment.

There is no doubt that he was illtreated; but if he had not been an ignorant man, he would not have pronounced against the cause of liberty on account of the treatment he received at the hands of individuals. But the savage in his nature was aroused, and he carried out his fierce threats to the fullest extent. For the time being, he attached himself to another American command; but at the first opportunity he deserted to the enemy, and became the scourge and terror of those who opposed the British cause. He spared none. His field extended from the Florida line to the Savannah River, in what is now Elbert County, and far into South Carolina. He appeared when least expected, and carried destruction with him. His mare became as noted as her master. In what was then Upper Georgia, she was known as "The Bald-faced Pony." On many an occasion he owed his life to the fleetness of his mare. But his vengeance was never satisfied: it was always active, and thirsting for the blood of the American patriot. The whim of the officer to possess McGirth's mare was a foolish one at best. It was the cause of great public and private suffering.

When South Carolina was rescued from the British,

McGirth retreated into Georgia, and finally into Florida. When the Spaniards regained possession of that territory, he became subject to their laws. For some reason or other he was thrown into one of the dungeons of the old fort at St. Augustine, where he was confined for five years. When released, his health was broken, and it was with great difficulty that he managed to return to Sumter District, in South Carolina, where his wife lived.

A very queer and eccentric character in the Revolution was Captain Rory McIntosh, of Mallow. Though Rory was a kinsman of General Lachlan and Colonel John McIntosh, who were among the most active Liberty Boys in Georgia, he took up arms for the King, and a very devoted Tory he was. His eccentricities would have been called whims if he had not stuck to them with such constancy. He was a Highlander and a follower of the Stuarts. How and why he became loyal to the new line of British kings, history does not state; but his clan had a chief, and he no doubt thought that every government ought to have a monarch. When the Revolution began, he was over sixty years of age, and was living comfortably on his plantation at Mallow; but he volunteered, and fought through the war.

A story is told of Rory McIntosh that once when the Spaniards held East Florida, he carried to St. Augustine a drove of cattle. He received payment in dollars, which he placed in a canvas bag behind him on his horse. When near his home, the bag gave way, and a part of the money fell out. He secured what was left and rode on, paying no attention to that which had fallen from the bag. When in need of money some years after, he returned to the place where the dollars had spilled, picked up as many as he wanted, and went back home. Whenever he could, he went about accompanied by a piper. Rory was a tall, finely formed man, with bristling whiskers and a ruddy complexion : consequently when he appeared on parade, he attracted great attention.

In 1778 two expeditions were sent from St. Augustine for the purpose of attacking Savannah, — one by sea, and one by land under command of Lieutenant Colonel Prevost. This land expedition had been joined by Captain Roderick McIntosh, in the capacity of a volunteer. He attached himself particularly to the infantry company commanded by Captain Murray. When the British laid siege to Sunbury and the fort, Captain Murray's company was in the line near the fort. One morning when Captain Rory had had a dram too much, he determined to sally out and summon the fort to surrender. His comrades tried to restrain him, but he was determined. Finally he strutted out, a drawn claymore in his hand, with his trusty slave Jim. He approached the fort and cried out, —

"Surrender, you miscreants! How dare you presume to resist his Majesty's arms?"

Colonel McIntosh, who commanded the fort, saw at once the condition of Captain Rory, and forbade the men to fire. Then he threw open the gate, and said, —

"Walk in, Mr. McIntosh, and take possession."

"No," cried Rory, "I'll not trust myself among such vermin. I order you to surrender!"

At that moment a rifle was fired by some one in the fort, and the ball passed through Captain Rory's face from side to side under the eyes. He fell backwards, but immediately recovered, and stood on his feet flourishing his claymore. Then he began to walk backward, his face to the fort. Several shots were fired at him, and Jim called out, —

"Run, massa, run! dey kill you!"

"Run!" cried Rory scornfully. "You may run, but I belong to a race that never runs!"

It was at the siege of Sunbury that Colonel McIntosh, when summoned by Colonel Prevost to surrender the fort, sent back the reply, "COME AND TAKE IT!"

AUNT NANCY HART.

THERE lived in Georgia, during the Revolutionary struggle, the most remarkable woman in some respects that the country has produced. To find her match, we shall have to go to the fables that are told about the Amazons. The Liberty Boys called her Aunt Nancy Hart. The Indians, struck by her wonderful feats in behalf of her country, called her "The War Woman;" and there is a creek in Elbert County, where she lived, that was named by the Indians "War Woman's Creek."

There are other heroines to whom history has paid more attention, and whose deeds have been celebrated in song and story; but not one of them was more devoted to the high cause of freedom, or more courageous, or depended less on aid from others, than Aunt Nancy Hart. In this last respect, the War Woman of Georgia stands alone in history, just as she stood alone when the Tories were waging a war of extermination, sparing neither women nor children, in the region in which she lived. Invention and fable have kindly come to the aid of the most famous of the world's heroines, but neither fable nor invention has touched the character or the deeds of this heroine of the Revolution. She stands out on the pages of history rough, uncouth, hot-tempered, unmanageable, uneducated, impolite, ugly, and sharp-tongued; but, as her friends said of her, "What a honey of a patriot she was!" She loved the Liberty Boys as well as she loved her own children. It has been said that she was cruel; but this charge may as well be put out of sight. Before passing upon it, we should have to know what the War Woman's eyes had seen, and what terrible revelations her ears had heard. Standing for American independence in a region that swarmed with Tories, whose murderous deeds never have been and never will be fully set forth, Aunt Nancy Hart had to defend her own hearthstone and her own children.

The maiden name of this remarkable woman was Morgan, and she was born in North Carolina. She married Benjamin Hart, a brother of Colonel Thomas Hart of Kentucky. Thomas Hart was the father of the wife of Henry Clay, and the uncle of the celebrated Thomas Hart Benton. Aunt Nancy and her husband moved to Georgia with the North Carolina emigrants, and settled on Broad River, in what is now Elbert County. She was nearly six feet high, and very muscular, — the result of hard work. She had red hair, and it is said that she was cross-eyed, but this has been denied on good authority. It matters little. Her eyes were keen enough to pierce through all Tory disguises, and that was enough for her. It is certain that her courage and her confidence kept alive the spark of liberty in hearts that would otherwise have smothered it, and was largely responsible for kindling it into the flame that finally swept the British out of that section, and subdued the Tories. When the Whigs and patriots who had been her neighbors were compelled to flee before the murderous Tories, she refused to go with them, but stood her ground and never ceased to speak her sentiments boldly. Nothing but the wholesome dread with which she had inspired them prevented the Tories from murdering her and her children. When General Elijah Clarke moved the women and children of the Broad River region to an asylum in Kentucky, and the Liberty Boys had taken refuge in South Carolina, Aunt Nancy Hart remained at home, and for a long and dismal period she was unprotected save by her own remarkable courage.

At that period the houses were built of logs, and the chimneys were built of sticks plastered with clay. They were called "stack chimneys." One evening Aunt Nancy and her children were sitting around the fire, on which a pot of soap was boiling. Now, a pot of soap must be constantly stirred, and for this the strong, muscular arms of Aunt Nancy were peculiarly fitted. So she stirred the soap, and, as she stirred, told the youngsters the latest news of the war. Presently one of her children chanced to discover some one peeping through the crack of the chimney, eavesdropping. By a gesture or a nod of the head Aunt Nancy was informed of what was going on. She smiled, and grew more spirited in her talk, rattling away and laughing as she gave exaggerated accounts of the recent defeats of the Tories. As she talked, she stirred the bubbling soap, and kept her keen eyes on the crack where the eavesdropper had been seen. Suddenly she dashed a ladleful of boiling soap through the crack full into the face of the intruder. It was so quickly and deftly done, that the eavesdropper had no time to dodge the scalding stuff. He received the full benefit of it. Blinded and half crazed by the pain, he howled and screamed at a tremendous rate. Aunt Nancy went out, and, after amusing herself at his expense, bound him fast and held him prisoner. The probability is that the next day she tucked up her petticoats, shouldered her gun, and compelled the unlucky Tory to ford the river ahead of her; and that, once on the other side, she kept in constant communication with the Clarkes and with other partisans of the American cause.

Her husband, whom she sometimes jokingly described as "a poor stick," assisted her in her communications. A conch shell was kept at the spring, some distance from the house. On this conch shell the children were taught to blow the blasts that gave Mr. Hart

information. One signal was, "The enemy is at hand;"
another was, "Keep close;" another, "Make tracks for
the swamp;" and still another was that he and his
friends were wanted at the cabin.

At the very darkest hour of the Revolution in
Georgia, Aunt Nancy performed one of her most remarkable feats, — one that brought into play all the
courage and devotion of her strong nature, and all the
tact and audacity that belonged to her character.

Brigadier General Andrew Williamson, with three
hundred men, was encamped near Augusta. When
Charleston fell, this officer, who was already a traitor,
though his treachery had not been avowed, called his
officers together, and expressed the opinion that it
would be foolish to further resist the King. He therefore advised them to return to their homes, and there
accept the protection which would be offered them.
He then abandoned his command, which was immediately disbanded. Shortly afterwards Colonels Brown
and Garrison, two partisans of the King's army who had
made themselves notorious by their cruelty to Americans, seized Augusta. Brown had been tarred and
feathered in Augusta just before the breaking-out of
the Revolution, and he made the patriots of that town
and of the country roundabout pay dearly for the indignities that had been heaped upon him on account of
his loyalty to the Crown. He confiscated the property
of the patriots, and issued an order banishing all Whig
families beyond the borders of Georgia.

Raiding parties were sent into the region in the
neighborhood of Augusta to compel the inhabitants to

take the oath of allegiance to the King. One of these parties entered the house of Colonel John Dooly, a gallant officer, and murdered him in cold blood in the presence of his wife and children. Colonel Dooly was the father of Judge Dooly, who became famous in Georgia after the war.

A detachment of this murdering party found its way to Aunt Nancy Hart's cabin. There were five Tories in the detachment, and Aunt Nancy received them coldly enough. They told her they had come to inquire into the truth of a report they had heard to the effect that she had aided a well-known rebel to escape from a company of King's men by whom he was pursued. With a twinkle of malice in her eyes, Aunt Nancy boldly declared that she had aided her Liberty Boy to escape, and then she described the affair.

She said that one day she heard the gallop of a horse. Looking out, she saw a horseman approaching, and at once knew him to be a Whig flying from pursuers. She let down the bars near her cabin, told him to ride his horse right through her house, in at the front door and out at the back, to take to the swamp, and hide himself the best he could. She then put up the bars, entered her house, closed the doors, and went about her business. In a little while a party of Tories rode up, and called to her with some rudeness. She muffled her head and face in a shawl, opened the door slowly, and asked in a feeble voice who it was that wanted to pester a sick, lone woman. The Tories said they had been pursuing a man, and had traced him near her house. They wanted to know if any one had passed that way. "I told 'em," said Aunt Nancy to the listening Tories, "that I had seen a man on a sorrel horse turn out of the road into the woods a little ways back. So they went back and took to the woods, and my Whig boy got off safe and sound."

Naturally this story, boldly told, did not please the five Tories who heard it; but something in the War Woman's eye prevented them from offering her any personal injury. Instead, they ordered her to give them something to eat.

"I never feed King's men if I can help it," she replied. "The scamps have fixed me so that I can't feed my own family in a decent manner. They have run off with all my pigs and poultry except that old gobbler you see in the yard there."

"Well, you shall cook the old gobbler for us," exclaimed one who seemed to be the leader of the party. Suiting the action to the word, he raised his musket and shot the gobbler. One of his men brought it into the house and gave it to Aunt Nancy, with orders to clean and cook it at once. This, of course, made that stanch patriot very angry, and she gave the Tories a violent tongue lashing.

It is probable that while she was dressing the turkey for the pot, the Tories let some hint drop about the outrageous murder of Colonel John Dooly, who was a warm friend of Aunt Nancy's. At any rate, she suddenly changed her tactics. She ceased to storm and quarrel, the scowl left her face, and she soon seemed to be in high good humor. She went about getting the meal ready with great good will. She sent her

little girl to the spring after water, but told her to
sound on the conch shell the signal to "keep close,"
so that her husband and his neighbors who were with
him might know there were Tories in the cabin.

While the daughter was gone after water, one of the
Tories volunteered to take her place in helping to get
everything ready. Aunt Nancy accepted his services,
and joked with him with great freedom and familiar-
ity. Like all women of spirit and independence, Aunt
Nancy possessed a considerable fund of humor, and it
stood her in good stead now. She contrived to thoroughly interest the Tories, and it was not long before
they were in the most jovial frame of mind imagina-
ble. They had expected to find a bad-tempered, ill-
conditioned woman; and they were agreeably surprised
when they found, instead, a woman who could match
their rude jests, and make herself thoroughly entertaining.

The Tories had brought a jug with them, and they
were so pleased with Aunt Nancy's seeming friendliness that they invited her to drink with them. "I'll
take one swig with you," said Aunt Nancy, "if it kills
every cow on the Island," meaning a neck of land at
the junction of river and creek where the Whig families of the neighborhood pastured their cattle and hid
them. The Tories laughed and drank, and then they
laughed and drank again. They kept this up until the
old gobbler had been cooked to Aunt Nancy's satisfaction; and by the time they were ready to sit down to
table they were in a very merry mood indeed.

They had stacked their arms within easy reach of

where they had been sitting and drinking; but Aunt Nancy had moved her table to the middle of the floor, so as to be able to walk around it on all sides while waiting on the Tories. In helping the men to the turkey and other eatables that she had prepared, she frequently came between them and their muskets. The Tories had hardly begun to eat before they called for water. Aunt Nancy, expecting this, had used up in cooking all that had been brought: consequently her daughter had to take the piggin and go to the spring after a fresh supply. She went with instructions to signal her father, and the neighbors who were with him, to come immediately to the cabin. While her daughter was at the spring, Aunt Nancy managed to pull off one of the boards that filled the space between the logs of the house, and through this crack she slipped two of the muskets. She was slipping the third through when her movements caught the eye of one of the Tories. Instantly the men sprang to their feet, but Aunt Nancy was now in her element. Quick as a flash she clapped the musket to her shoulder, and threatened to shoot the first man that approached her. The men, knowing her reputation as a fighter, and awed by her appearance, hesitated. At last one bolder than the rest began to advance toward her. She fired promptly, and at the report of the gun the man fell dead on the floor.

Before the others could recover from their consternation, Aunt Nancy had seized another musket, and held it in readiness to fire again. Her daughter had now returned from the spring with the information that her father and his neighbors would soon arrive. Directed by her mother, the girl took the remaining musket and carried it out of the house. The Tories, seeing that no time was to be lost in recovering their arms, proposed to rush upon Aunt Nancy in a body

and overpower her. But the War Woman was equal to the occasion. She fired again, and brought down another Tory. As she did so, the daughter, acting on her orders, handed her another musket. Then, taking position in the doorway, she called on the men to "surrender their ugly Tory carcasses to a Whig woman."

The Tories agreed to surrender, and wanted to shake hands to make the bargain binding; but Aunt Nancy kept her position in the doorway until her husband and his friends made their appearance. The Whigs wanted to shoot the Tories; but Aunt Nancy, whose blood was up, declared that shooting was too good for them. "They've murdered John Dooly," she exclaimed; "now let them hang for it!" Thereupon the Tories were taken out and hanged. The tree from which they swung was still standing as late as 1838, and was often pointed out by old people who had lived through the troubled times of the Revolution.

One day Aunt Nancy met a Tory going along the highway. She engaged him in conversation, diverted his attention, and suddenly seized his gun and wrenched it away from him. She then ordered him to take up the line of march for a fort not far distant. Not daring to disobey, the man marched before her, as many others had been compelled to do, and she turned him over to the commander of the fort.

When Augusta was in the hands of the British, and their raiding parties had been driven in by the Americans under Colonel Elijah Clarke, it became necessary for that commander to get some positive information in regard to the intentions of the British. At this juncture Aunt Nancy came to the rescue. She disguised herself as a man, and went boldly into the British camp. She remained there for several days, pretending to be crazy. In this way she secured a great deal of important information, and made haste to carry it to Colonel Clarke.

Aunt Nancy was once left in a fort with several other women and a number of small children, her own among the rest. The men had gone out in search of supplies. They had not expected an attack, and had left only one of their number, a young man, to protect the women and children. Suddenly a party of Tories and Indians made its appearance, and surrounded the fort, which was nothing more than a stockade. The yelling of the savages threw all the women and children into the utmost confusion, — all except Aunt Nancy. That wonderful woman, who never knew what fear was, only became more energetic in the face of danger. There was a small cannon in the fort, but it was not in position to reach the enemy with its fire. After trying her best to lift the cannon into position, Aunt Nancy remembered the young man who had been left in the fort, and looked about for him; but he was not to be seen. A close search discovered him hiding under a cowhide. Aunt Nancy pulled him out by the heels, and vowed she would make mince-meat of him unless he helped her to move the cannon. The fellow knew perfectly well that Aunt Nancy was not to be trifled with when her blood was up. He gave her the necessary assistance. She aimed the cannon and fired it, and the Tories and savages promptly took to their heels.

On another occasion when the river was high, it became necessary for the Americans on the Georgia side to know what was going on on the Carolina side; but no one could be induced to venture across. Hearing of the difficulty, Aunt Nancy promptly undertook to go.

The freshet had swept away all the boats, but to Aunt Nancy this was a trifling matter. She found a few logs, tied them together with grapevines, and on this raft made the voyage across the river. She gathered the necessary information, and made haste to communicate it to the Georgia troops.

Aunt Nancy was the mother of eight children, — six sons and two daughters. Her eldest daughter, Sally, married a man named Thompson, who was as quick-tempered as his mother-in-law. After the war, Aunt Nancy moved to Brunswick. Sally and her husband followed a year or two later. In passing through Burke County, they camped for the night by the roadside. The next morning Thompson ordered a white man, who had been hired as a teamster, to perform some duty. Thompson's tone was so peremptory that the man returned an insolent answer, and refused. In a fit of rage, Thompson drew his sword, and severed the man's head from his body with one swinging stroke. He then drove the team himself until he came to the first house, where he gave information that he had cut off a fellow's head at the camp down the road, and that they "had best go and bury him." He then drove on, but was overtaken, arrested, and lodged in jail at Waynesboro. As soon as Aunt Nancy heard of the trouble, she made her appearance in the upcountry again. Within a few days after her return, the jail was found open one morning, and Thompson was gone. Speaking of this afterwards, Aunt Nancy was heard to exclaim, —

"Drat 'em! that's the way with 'em all. When they get into trouble, they always send for me!"

STO. OF GA. — 6

Not long after this episode, Mr. Benjamin Hart died. Aunt Nancy mourned his loss for a while, and then married a young man. Then, as the saying is, she "pulled up stakes," and moved to what is now the State of Alabama, on the Tombigbee. There she had the French and the Spaniards for neighbors, and she felt at home with neither race. She was bluntly, emphatically, and unaffectedly American. To add to her troubles, a big rain flooded the river, destroyed her crops, and surrounded her house. This, with the French and Spaniards, was too much for her. She returned to Georgia, but, finding her old home occupied by others, she settled in Edgefield, S.C.

A Methodist society was formed in her neighborhood, and its influence became so active that Aunt Nancy's conscience began to trouble her. She listened to the preaching of the Word from a distance until she became worried about her future state. She went to the meetinghouse, but found the door closed against intruders. The deacon and members were holding a class meeting. The closed door was no obstacle to Aunt Nancy. She cut the fastening and walked in without ceremony. Once in, she found what she wanted. She became an enthusiastic Methodist, and is said to have fought Satan and sin as manfully as she fought the Tories and the British.

When Governor George R. Gilmer of Georgia was in Congress, in 1828–29, the members were very anxious to attract the notice of General Jackson, who had been elected President. A proposal was made to fill the vacant niches in the rotunda with paintings descriptive of the battle of New Orleans and the general's other victories. Governor Gilmer offered as an amendment a resolution to fill one of the niches with a painting of Aunt Nancy Hart wading Broad River, her petticoats held up with one hand, a musket in the other, and driving three Tories before her, to deliver them up to Colonel Elijah Clarke.

Governor Gilmer's proposition was a more sensible one than he intended it to be. Georgia has perpetuated Aunt Nancy's name by calling a county after her; but the Republic owes something to her memory.

TWO SOLDIERS OF THE REVOLUTION.

THE pen of the historian is not always as impartial as it should be. It has its spites and prejudices; and it frequently happens that the men who wield the pen with which history is written, have their whims, their likes, and their dislikes. It is certain that two of the hardest fighters in the War for Independence — two of the most distinguished officers that Georgia gave to the cause — have had tardy justice done to their valor. The names of these men are General James Jackson and General Elijah Clarke. The independence and the individuality of these men stand clearly out in all the records that we have of them, and it is no doubt true that these qualities made them to some degree unpopular with those who inspired the early chroniclers of the Revolution in the South. Neither of these officers was capable of currying favor with his superiors, or of doing injustice to the humblest of his comrades. They were not seekers after the bubble reputation, but had their minds and all their energies bent on liberating Georgia and her sister Colonies.

General James Jackson was born in the county of Devon, England. He came to this country in 1772, landing at Savannah penniless and almost friendless. He began the study of law; but when the Liberty Boys began their movement for resisting British oppression, he placed his books on their shelves, and gave himself entirely to the cause of the people. When only nineteen years old, he was one of the volunteers that fired the British armed vessels sent to attack Savannah by water, while Major Maitland and Major Grant attacked it by land. The crews of these vessels were compelled to escape without their clothes and arms. General Jackson served in the lower part of Georgia until the fall of Savannah in 1778, when he and his friend John Milledge made their way to the patriot troops, commanded by General Moultrie. Such was the condition of these men, both of whom afterwards became governors of Georgia, that they were compelled to make the greater part of their journey barefoot and in rags. Their appearance was so much against them that they were arrested as spies by some American soldiers, and would have been hanged but for the timely arrival of a gentleman who knew them.

General Jackson was at the siege of Savannah, and, after the disastrous result of that affair, returned to South Carolina. The victory of the Americans at Blackstock's House, in South Carolina, was almost wholly due to the Georgians who were there. Sumter commanded at the beginning of the action, but a severe wound compelled him to retire from the field. The command then devolved upon the oldest Georgia officer, General John Twiggs, who was assisted by Jackson, Clarke, and Chandler. In this engagement Tarleton, the famous leader of the British dragoons, was defeated for the first time, and he was never able to recover the prestige he had lost. Tarleton fled from the field, and Jackson was ordered to pursue him. It was owing only to the fleetness of his horse that Tarleton escaped.

At the battle of The Cowpens, Jackson again distinguished himself. "Major Jackson," says General Andrew Pickens, "by his example, and firm, active conduct, did much to animate the soldiers and insure the success of the day. He ran the utmost risk of his life in seizing the colors of the 71st British Regiment, and afterwards introducing Major McArthur, commanding officer of the British Infantry, as a prisoner of war to General Morgan." His services brought him to the attention of General Greene, and he was sent on a tour of difficult duty through North Carolina. He was so successful in this, that the commanding general authorized him to raise a partisan legion of infantry and cavalry for service in Georgia. By means of his native eloquence, which was said to be almost irresistible, he succeeded in raising the legion in a very short time. Wherever he addressed the people, there were loud cries of "Liberty and Jackson forever!" When his legion had been organized, he was appointed lieutenant colonel. His dragoons were clothed and armed by themselves, with the exception of their pistols. Their coats were made of dressed deerskins, and faced with the little blue that could be procured.

Just before the siege of Augusta, Jackson was called upon to employ his eloquence in preventing the militia from giving up in despair and returning to their homes. These men were utterly worn out. Being ignorant men, they could see no ray of hope. They lacked every necessary of life. Jackson roused their drooping spirits, restored their hopes, and revived their old-time enthusiasm. At the siege of Augusta these men fought fiercely. Jackson himself led one of the advance parties. After the surrender of the town, he was ordered to level the fortifications, and he was appointed commandant. He was afterwards ordered to take position midway between Augusta and Savannah. While he held this position, a conspiracy was formed in the infantry to kill him in his bed. A soldier named Davis, who waited in the commander's tent, suspected that something was wrong. So he mingled among the men, and applied many harsh epithets to Jackson. Thinking to make Davis useful to them, the conspirators told him their plans, which he made haste to lay before his superior officer. Shortly afterwards the infantry were drawn up in line, and the ringleaders in the conspiracy arrested, tried, and executed.

After the war the Legislature gave Davis a horse, saddle, and bridle, and five hundred acres of land, as a reward for his fidelity.

Jackson was with General Wayne in his Georgia campaign, and was intrusted by him with many hazardous duties. When Savannah surrendered, General Wayne issued an order in which he said, " Lieutenant Colonel Jackson, in consideration of his severe and fatiguing service in the advance, is to receive the key of Savannah, and is allowed to enter the western gate."

In 1786, Jackson was made brigadier general, and had command of the forces operating against the Indians. Between 1788 and 1806 General Jackson held almost every high office within the gift of the people of the State, — member of the Legislature, governor when only thirty-one years old, member of the first Congress held under the Federal Constitution, member of the State Constitutional Convention, presidential elector, and United States senator.

With General Jackson in many of his engagements was General Elijah Clarke, who in many respects was the most remarkable soldier that Georgia contributed to the War for Independence. With fairer opportunities than he had, he would have made a great commander. He had small knowledge of tactics, but he had what is better, — the skill to take advantage of quickly passing events, and the coolness that made him complete master of all his resources. He was a man of the most striking characteristics, and he came out of the war with many bitter enemies among those with whom he came in contact. This feeling was perpetuated by the political campaigns in which his son, John Clarke, took part after the war. A trace of this is to be seen in the sketch which Governor Gilmer gives to Elijah Clarke in his curious book entitled "Georgians." It is undoubtedly true that Elijah Clarke was ignorant of what is called book knowledge, but he was not much worse off in this respect than the famous Confederate General Forrest, who is thought by some high military critics to have been the most remarkable commander on the Southern side in the civil war. Elijah Clarke, as well as General Forrest, had something that served them a better turn than a mere knowledge of books. They had a thorough knowledge of men, and a quick eye for the situations that follow each other so rapidly in a skirmish or battle.

Elijah Clarke was born in North Carolina, but moved to Georgia in 1774. He was among the first of the inhabitants of Upper Georgia to take up the cause of American independence; and his example, for he was a notable man even in private life, did much to solidify and strengthen those who leaned to that cause. When the British troops marched from the coast into Upper Georgia, Elijah thought the time had come to take his gun from the rack over the door, and make at least some show of resistance. His courage, and the firmness and decision of his character, made him the natural leader of those of his neighbors whose sympathies were with the Liberty Boys in other parts of the State, and he soon found himself a commander without commission or title. He cared less for these things than for the principles of liberty for which he was fighting.

For a while Elijah Clarke and his followers fought as partisan rangers, but he soon drew around him a compact and disciplined body of men who were ready to go wherever he might lead them. He did not confine his efforts to his new neighborhood. We hear of him with Howe's ill-fated expedition against East Florida, where, at Alligator Creek, he was asked to perform the impossible feat of storming with a troop of horse a camp intrenched behind logs and brushwood. He was no doubt amazed at the stupidity of General Howe in issuing such an order, but he attempted to carry it out with his usual courage. He did succeed in floundering over the logs with his troops, but he came to a ditch that was too wide for his horses to leap, and too deep to be ridden through. At this moment he and his men were saluted with a heavy fire from the enemy, and they were compelled to retire in confusion. In this attempt Elijah Clarke was shot through the thigh. Later he was in South Carolina, at Blackstocks, and at The Cowpens.

In some quarters an effort has been made to blacken the reputation of General Clarke by comparing his treatment of the Tories with the mild and humane policy pursued by Francis Marion. There was, indeed, some misunderstanding between the two men in regard to the methods that might be adopted. The policy of Marion was undoubtedly the correct one, so far as South Carolina was concerned; but if the Tories in that Province had been guilty of the crimes committed by their brethren in Wilkes and the surrounding region, General Marion's policy would not have been very different from that of General Clarke. The Tories with whom Clarke was familiar were guilty of murder, rapine, pillage, and incendiarism. The Tories in South Carolina were kept under by the presence of Marion and his men. Clarke went wherever his services were needed; and during his absence, the Tories of the Broad River region were free to commit every excess. Marion refused to leave the region where he made his name famous, and thus kept the Tories in constant fear and dread.

Who shall say that Marion would not have been

as ready to exterminate the Tories as Clarke was, or
that Clarke would not have been as humane as Marion,
if each of these distinguished patriots had been in the
other's place?

At the battle of Kettle Creek, in what is now Wilkes
County, Elijah Clarke distinguished himself by his
readiness and skill as a commander. The Americans
under Colonel Pickens were in pursuit of the British
under Colonel Boyd. Their line of march was the
order of battle, and following the vanguard came the
right and left wings. The left wing was commanded
by Elijah Clarke. The center was led by Colonel
Pickens, who was in command of the expedition.
Colonel Boyd, the British commander, appeared to be
unconscious of pursuit. He had halted on a farm on
the north side of Kettle Creek. His horses were left to
forage on the young cane that grew on the edge of the
swamp; and his men were slaying cattle and parching
corn, preparing for a feast after their short rations.
The British encampment was formed near the creek,
on a piece of open ground flanked on two sides by a
canebrake. Colonel Boyd was in utter ignorance of
the approach of the Americans, who advanced at once
to the attack. The British colonel formed his line in
the rear of his encampment, and there received the
assault. The battle was hotly contested for more than
an hour, and then the Tories retreated through the
swamp.

Elijah Clarke, seeing a piece of rising ground on the
farther side of the creek, on which he suspected the
Loyalists would try to form, ordered the left wing to

follow him, and was about to cross the stream when his horse was shot under him. Mounting another, he soon crossed the creek, followed by not more than a fourth of his division. There had been some mistake in sending the order along the line. Clarke gained the hill that had attracted his eye just in time to attack Major Spurgen, a brave British officer, who was forming his command. The firing attracted the notice of the rest of Clarke's division, and they soon joined their leader. Pickens and Dooly also pressed through the swamp, and the battle was renewed with great vigor. For a while the result was in doubt, but at the end the Americans held the hill. The Tories fled in all directions, leaving seventy dead on the field, and seventy-five wounded and captured. Of the Americans, nine were slain, and twenty-three wounded. To Elijah Clarke must be given the credit for this victory, which, coming at the time it did, revived the hopes and courage of the Liberty Boys in all parts of the country.

The Tories, on the other hand, were so depressed by it, that many of them left that part of the State, and those who remained became comparatively quiet. The situation was so encouraging, that many of the people of Georgia, who had been driven from their homes by the cruelty of the Tories, returned with their families. They were not long left in peace, however. The British and the Tories had their active agents among the Creeks and Cherokees, urging these tribes to take up arms and attack the Americans. In view of this, Clarke was sent to guard the frontier forts. Then the Tories again began to pillage and devastate the Broad River

region. Some of the crimes they committed would
have disgraced savages. Clarke's house was burned,
and his family ordered to leave the State. Mrs. Clarke
and her two daughters started on their perilous journey
with nothing but a small pony of little value, and even
this was taken from them before they had gone very
far. This only served to renew the activity of Clarke
in behalf of the American cause. He defeated the
Tories wherever he met them; and if he gave them no
quarter, it was because they had shown no mercy to
the Americans. The savage character of the warfare
waged by the Tories against men, women, and children,
must ever stand as an explanation and as an excuse for
the fierce spirit displayed by Clarke and the Americans
who lived in the Broad River region.

In the battle near Musgrove's Mill, Clarke defeated
the British, killing sixty-three men, and wounding and
capturing one hundred. During the battle he was twice
severely wounded on the head and neck; and once he
was surrounded by the enemy, captured, and placed in
charge of two men. One of these he knocked down with
a blow of his fist, and the other fled. At one time, acting without orders, he was near taking Augusta, and was
only prevented by the desire of his men to see their families. After this he returned to Wilkes County, where he
was compelled to take under his protection nearly four
hundred women and children who had been driven from
their homes by the savage Tories. He resolved to carry
these to a place of safety, and, with a sufficient guard,
set out for Kentucky. Cornwallis, hearing of this movement, and taking for granted that it was a retreat, sent

one hundred men under Captain Ferguson to cut Clarke off, the supposition being that the great partisan fighter would march through South Carolina, but he had re-crossed the mountains in the Piedmont region. Hearing of this movement, Clarke detached Major Chandler and Captain Johnston with thirty men to take part in the operations against Ferguson. Thus it was the pursuit of Clarke that brought on the memorable battle of Kings Mountain, which resulted in a great victory for the cause of American independence; and although Clarke was not there in person, his heroic spirit animated the brave men who won the day.

He was the first to teach the militia to stand against the bayonets of the British; and at Blackstocks, in South Carolina, at the head of his Wilkes riflemen, he charged and drove the British light infantry in an open field, — a movement that turned the enemy's right flank, and insured the victory of the Americans. At the siege of Augusta, Clarke had anticipated the movement of Colonel "Light Horse Harry" Lee, and had confined the British garrison to their works for weeks before Colonel Lee's arrival.

At the close of the Revolution, Clarke led the movement against the Indians. He defeated the Creeks in the battle of Jacks Creek. After peace was declared, Clarke, who had been made a general by a grateful State, settled on lands that had been reserved to the Indians. For this he has been criticised very severely; but it is curious that the policy for which he was attacked, shortly afterwards became the policy of the whole people. The States and the United States have made treaties with the Indians, only to break them. Having personal knowledge of the Indians, and having been made the victim of some of their raids, he had no respect for them or for their rights. To this view the whole country afterwards came, and the red men disappeared before it.

It will be well to bear in mind, that, whatever failings he may have had, there was not a more heroic figure in the Revolution than General Elijah Clarke.

A WAR OF EXTERMINATION.

SOME of the barbarous features of the Revolutionary War in Georgia have been briefly noted. History has turned her eyes away from the more horrible details; but by reading between the lines, and taking advantage of the hints and suggestions, it is not hard to get a tolerably fair idea of the methods that were pursued on both sides. Even Colonel Charles C. Jones, jun., whose "History of Georgia" is thus far the most complete that has been written, touches lightly on the cruelties practiced in the efforts of the British and

Tories to wrest Upper Georgia from the control of the Americans. There are matters that History cannot deal with and maintain her dignity.

There can be no doubt that the British and the Tories began their cruelties without considering the results to which their acts would lead. It is an easy matter at this late day to see how naturally the war, in the region tributary to Augusta, degenerated into a series of crimes and barbarities foul enough to cause History to hold her hands before her eyes. When Colonel Campbell, assisted by Colonel Brown, advanced to attack Augusta, it was the only American post that had not surrendered to the King's men, and its capture would complete the subjugation of Georgia from a military point of view. The city fell without a struggle, and the American forces retreated across the river. It was natural that the British, and the Tories who were acting with them, should take advantage of this victory to bring the whole region above and around Augusta to terms. The sooner this was done, the sooner would all Georgia be restored to her relations with his Majesty George III. No time was to be lost. Therefore Colonel Campbell, the British commander, tarried in Augusta but a few days. He left Colonel Brown in charge, and marched in the direction of Wilkes County. Those of the inhabitants who had Tory sympathies were to be encouraged; but those who were disaffected were to be dealt with summarily, so as to put an end, at once and forever, to the disloyalty that had been active in that region. This plan was carried out promptly and violently. The severest punishment was the portion of those who refused to take the oath of allegiance. Plunder and the torch were the portions of those who chanced to be away from home, fighting for their country. Their helpless wives and children were left homeless, and destitute of provisions. Fortunately a great many stanch Liberty Boys had carried their families, their household effects, and their cattle, into South Carolina as soon as they heard of the fall of Augusta; but many had remained at home, and the sufferings of these were severe.

Another explanation of the extreme cruelty with which the war in Upper Georgia was waged after the fall of Augusta, was the fact that Colonel Brown, who had been left in command by Colonel Campbell, had some old scores to settle. At the very beginning of the struggle he had been arrested in Augusta by some of the Liberty Boys, tarred and feathered, and paraded through the public streets, on account of his outspoken loyalty to the King. Still another reason was the fact that Daniel McGirth, who had been maltreated by an American officer, was among the officers who had accompanied Colonel Brown. McGirth held every American responsible for the treatment he had received, and he spared few that fell into his hands. Thus, between the anxiety of the British to conquer Georgia completely, and the desires of Brown and McGirth to revenge themselves, the Americans in Upper Georgia were made the victims of the most inhuman barbarities.

The Americans under Elijah Clarke lost no time in retaliating, and thus was begun a contest that may be aptly described as a war of extermination. Clarke was enabled to defeat the British and the Tories wherever they opposed him on anything like equal terms, and this fact added to the rigor with which they treated the Americans who were so unfortunate as to fall into their hands. Shortly after the affair at Musgrove's Mill, in which Clarke defeated the British and the Tories, Lord Cornwallis addressed a circular letter to the officers commanding the advanced posts. He declared, "The inhabitants of the Provinces who have subscribed to and taken part in this revolt shall be punished with the utmost rigor; and also those who will not turn out shall be imprisoned, and their whole property taken from them or destroyed. I have ordered," he goes on to say, "in the most positive manner, that every militia-man who has borne arms with us, and afterwards joined the enemy, shall be immediately hanged. I desire you will take the most vigorous measures to punish the rebels in the district in which you command, and that you obey in the strictest manner the directions I have given in this letter relative to the inhabitants in this country."

Here was authority broad enough to cover every crime that the British and the Tories might see fit to commit, and they stretched it to the utmost limit. They burned houses and destroyed property. They insulted and inhumanly treated women and children. They hanged the innocent. They went about the country practicing every barbarity that their savage and bloodthirsty natures could suggest. It was no wonder that the Americans retaliated whenever they had the opportunity. It was no wonder that Elijah Clarke, naturally independent and irritable, should fail to see the

justice or necessity of treating the Tories he captured
as prisoners of war.

The situation of the Americans became so serious
that Clarke determined to strike a heavy blow.   He
returned from Carolina to Wilkes County in September,
1780, and in two days succeeded in placing in the field
three hundred and fifty men.   With this force, strengthened by eighty men recruited in Carolina, he boldly
marched on Augusta.   The movement was so unexpected, that, but for the fact that the advance guard
fell in with an Indian camp which it was compelled to
attack, Colonel Brown would have been taken completely by surprise.   But the retreating Indians gave
him notice, and he took refuge with his command in a
strong building known as the White House.   The siege
began on the 14th.   By daylight on the 16th Clarke
had succeeded in cutting the garrison off from its water
supply.   The sufferings of the men, especially the
wounded, became most intense.   The Americans could
hear their cries for water and for medical aid.   Brown
appears to have been as brave as he was cruel.   Though
he was shot through both thighs, he remained at the
head of his men ; and his great courage sustained the
spirits of his followers.   Clarke summoned him to surrender on the 17th.   He not only refused, but warned
the American commander that the demonstration he
was making against the King's men would bring destruction to the western part of Georgia.

Meanwhile some of Clarke's men had gone to visit
their families, and others were more interested in securing plunder than in forwarding the cause of independ-

ence. Colonel Brown, as soon as he heard of the approach of the Americans, had sent several messengers by different routes to inform Colonel Cruger of the state of affairs. Cruger, who was in Carolina at Ninety-six, promptly set his men in motion, and on the morning of the 18th appeared on the bank of the Savannah, opposite Augusta. Under the circumstances, Clarke was compelled to retreat. He had suffered a loss of sixty, killed and wounded. In retreating, he was compelled to leave twenty-nine of his wounded men behind. Among these was Captain Ashby, one of the bravest and most humane of the officers of the American army. This unfortunate officer and the men with him fell into the hands of the enemy. Colonel Brown was so severely wounded that he was unable to move about; so he ordered Captain Ashby and twelve of the wounded prisoners to be hanged on the staircase of the White House, where he might see their sufferings and gloat over their agonies. These men were cruelly strangled before Brown's eyes. But their fate was a happy one compared with that of their wounded companions. Those men were turned over to the red savages, who were the allies of the British. The Indians received the prisoners with howls of delight, and began at once to torture them in every conceivable way. They formed a circle, and marched around the Americans, cutting and slashing them with their knives. The end of the unfortunates was most horrible. They were ripped with knives, scalped, and then burned. No doubt, Colonel Brown enjoyed this scene more thoroughly than he did the tame and commonplace spectacle of strangling Captain Ashby and his companions.

Before raising the siege, Elijah Clarke paroled the officers and men whom he had captured,—fifty-six men, all told. This fact is mentioned to show that the Georgia militia had not then begun those acts of retaliation which have attracted the notice of historians. They had had, as we know, abundant provocation; but after the horrible crimes perpetrated by Brown reached their ears, they threw off all restraint. Self-preservation is the first law of nature, and the men who acted with Elijah Clarke thought that the best way to preserve the lives of themselves and their families was to destroy the Tories as fast as they caught them. The fact is chronicled by Colonel Johes, and it is worth noting, that the officers and men paroled by Clarke, in utter disregard of their obligations, took up their arms as soon as the Americans had departed. The probability is that they were driven to this by the commands of Brown.

It is well known, that, as soon as Clarke and his men had retreated, Colonel Brown sent detachments of troops in all directions, with orders to arrest all persons who had taken part in the siege, or who had sympathized with the efforts of the Americans to recapture Augusta. Under this sweeping order, men of all ages and conditions were dragged from their homes and thrown into prison. Those who were suspected of taking part in the siege, or of belonging to Clarke's command, were seized and hanged out of hand. Old men, no longer able to bear arms, were imprisoned for welcoming the return of members of their families who had fought on the American side. One instance out of many that might be cited was the arrest of the father of Captains Samuel and James Alexander. In the seventy-eighth

year of his age, this old man was arrested at his home, tied to the tail of a cart, and dragged forty miles in two days. When caught leaning against the cart to rest his feeble limbs, he was whipped by the driver. It was at this time that in the region round about Augusta the hopes of the patriots grew very faint. The women and children assembled, and begged Elijah Clarke to take them out of the country; and in response to the appeals of these defenseless ones, he undertook the movement that culminated in the glorious victory of Kings Mountain.

The winter of 1780 was the darkest hour of the Revolution in Upper Georgia. There was no trade. Farming was at a low ebb. The schoolhouses were closed. Many of the patriots had carried off their families. Many had gone with Elijah Clarke to Kentucky. The patriots had betaken themselves to South Carolina, though the services they rendered there have been slurred over by the historians of that State.

When General Greene began his Southern campaign, and gradually rid South Carolina of the British and the Tory element, the patriots of Upper Georgia ventured to return to their homes. Captain McCall, who was among them, says, in his history, that they returned in parties of ten and twelve, so as to attract as little attention as possible. They appointed Dennis's Mill, on Little River, as a place of meeting. "When these small parties entered the settlements where they had formerly lived," says Captain McCall, "general devastation was presented to view; their aged fathers and their youthful brothers had been murdered; their decrepit grandfathers were incarcerated in prisons where most of them had been suffered to perish in filth, famine, or disease; and their mothers, wives, sisters, and young children had been robbed, insulted, and abused, and were found by them in temporary huts more resembling a savage camp than a civilized habitation." Though Captain McCall was an eyewitness of some of the scenes he describes, the picture he draws might seem to be too highly colored were it not supplemented by a great mass of evidence. One more instance out of many may be given. In a skirmish with the Americans under Colonel Harden, Brown captured several prisoners. Among them was a youth only seventeen years old named Rannal McKay, the son of a widow who was a refugee from Darien. Being told that her son was a prisoner in the hands of Brown, Widow McKay, providing herself with some refreshments that she thought might suit the taste of the British commander, went to Brown's headquarters, and begged that her son might be set free. The cruel wretch accepted the present she had brought him, but refused even to let her see her son, and caused the sentinels to put her out of the camp by force. Next day young McKay and four other prisoners were taken out of the rail pen in which they had been confined. By Brown's order they were hanged upon a gallows until they were nearly strangled. They were then cut down and turned over to the tender mercies of the Indians, by whom they were mutilated, scalped, and finally murdered in the most savage manner.

The cruelty of Colonel Brown and the Tories acting under him was so unbearable that the patriots of that region felt that their existence depended on the capture of Augusta. They decided on an aggressive movement when they met again at Dennis's Mill, on Little River.

Colonel Clarke, who was suffering from the results of smallpox, was too feeble to lead them. His place was taken for the time by Lieutenant Colonel Micajah Williamson; and on the 16th of April, 1781, the Americans moved to the vicinity of Augusta. They were there reënforced by a detachment from southern Georgia under Colonel Baker, and by a number of recruits from Burke County. A few days afterwards they were joined by some Carolina militiamen under Colonel Hammond and Major Jackson.

With this force, Colonel Williamson took up a position twelve hundred yards from the British works, and fortified his camp. The Americans were compelled to wait nearly a month for the aid they expected from General Greene. The militia, worn out with waiting for the reënforcements, were about to withdraw from the camp in despair, when Jackson, that truly great Georgian, made them an address full of the most passionate and patriotic eloquence, and this appeal changed their purpose. Jackson's voice was afterwards heard in the halls of Congress; but we may be sure that he was never more in earnest or more truly eloquent than when he pleaded with the faint-hearted Americans to stand to their cause and their arms. Jackson's address revived their courage; and when, on the 15th of May, Elijah Clarke rode into camp, restored to health and accompanied by one hundred fresh recruits, the confidence of the militiamen was fully renewed.

It was at this time that General Pickens and " Light Horse Harry " Lee (the father of General Robert E. Lee) were ordered by General Greene to march on

Augusta and capture that post. When Lee reached
the neighborhood of Augusta, he learned, from a party
of light horse which he had sent on ahead to collect
prisoners and gain information, that the annual royal
present intended for the Indians had arrived at Fort
Galphin, some distance below Augusta. The present
comprised blankets, liquor, salt, small arms, powder,
and ball. There was a great lack of these articles in
the American camp, and Lee resolved to capture them.
The supplies were so valuable, that Brown, the British
commander, had sent two companies from Augusta to
garrison Fort Galphin. This was the situation when
"Light Horse Harry" arrived on the ground. The
British in Augusta had not yet discovered his approach,
and promptness was necessary. Leaving Eaton's battalion, the artillery, and the footsore men of the legion,
to follow more slowly, Lee mounted a detachment of
infantry behind his dragoons, and made a forced march
to Fort Galphin.

This point he reached on the 21st of May, 1781.
The weather was extremely hot, and for miles the
troopers and their horses had been unable to find a
drop of water: consequently neither the men nor the
animals were in a condition to make the attack when
the command was brought to a halt under the pines
that skirted the field surrounding the fort. The British
within the fort were resting quietly, and were not aware
that an enemy was at hand. A prompt and decisive
movement was necessary; and when his men and
horses had rested a little while, Lee dismounted the
militiamen he had brought with him, and ordered them

to make a demonstration against the fort on the side opposite the position he had taken. This famous commander reasoned, that, as soon as the militiamen appeared before the fort, the garrison would sally from the stockade. The militia would retreat, the garrison pursuing, and he would seize upon that moment to assault and capture the post left defenseless. To carry out this plan, Captain Rudolph (who was supposed to be some great general in disguise), with a detachment of picked infantry, was held in readiness to rush upon the fort; while the rest of the troops, supported by the dragoons, were placed where they could shield the militia from the pursuit of the British.

The affair took place just as Lee had foreseen. The garrison sallied out to the attack. The militia, before making a show of resistance, began a retreat. The garrison gave pursuit. Captain Rudolph dashed across the field, and captured the fort without any trouble. The end came, when the militia rallied, and the foot soldiers and dragoons closed around the soldiers of the garrison. During the engagement the Americans lost one man from sunstroke. The enemy lost only three or four men. The rest, together with the valuable stores in the stockade, fell into the hands of the patriots.

Following this successful affair, which was of more importance than it seems now to be, Lee formed a junction with General Pickens; and these two then joined their forces with those of Clarke, who commanded the Georgia militia, and the siege of Augusta began. The first movement was the capture of Fort

Grierson, so called in honor of the man who commanded its garrison. Grierson, hard pressed, threw
open the gates of the fort, and endeavored to escape.
Thirty of his men were killed, and forty-five wounded
and captured. Grierson was made a prisoner, but was
killed by a Georgia rifleman. He was as cruel and
vindictive as Brown himself. He was a monster who
had made himself odious to the followers of Clarke.
In his history, Captain McCall strongly hints that
Grierson was shot by one of the sons of the aged
Mr. Alexander, who had been made prisoner and
dragged to Augusta tied to the tail of a cart. A
reward was offered for information that would lead
to the arrest of the man who shot Grierson, but the
reward was never claimed. The whole army probably
knew who had fired the fatal shot, and no doubt the
commanders knew, but their knowledge was not official.
No further notice was taken of the matter.

The capture of Fort Grierson cheered the hearts of
the besiegers, and gave them renewed courage. Fort
Cornwallis was next invested. This stronghold was
commanded by Colonel Brown himself, who was as bold
as he was cruel. He was mean enough to expose to
the American fire the aged Mr. Alexander and other
unfortunate patriots who had long been held as prisoners. Captain Samuel Alexander commanded one of
the companies close to the fort, and could see and
recognize his venerable father, who had been placed
in an exposed position by Brown.

It is not necessary to describe all the events of the
siege. Brown held out as long as he could, but was

finally compelled to surrender. On the 5th of June, 1781, Brown, with three hundred men, marched out of Fort Cornwallis, and that stronghold was immediately taken possession of by Captain Rudolph. A strong guard was detailed by the American commanders, to protect Brown from the just anger of the Georgia soldiers, under Clarke, Williamson, and Jackson. To insure his safety, he was carried to the quarters of "Light Horse Harry" Lee. The next day he and a few of his officers were paroled and sent down the river in charge of a party of infantry instructed to guard him. Ramsay, in his "History of the Revolution of South Carolina," says that Brown was recognized at Silver Bluff by Mrs. McKay, who thus addressed him: "Colonel Brown, in the late day of your prosperity I visited your camp, and on my knees supplicated for the life of my son; but you were deaf to my entreaties. You hanged him, though a beardless youth, before my face. These eyes have seen him scalped by the savages under your immediate command, and for no better reason than that his name was McKay. As you are now prisoner to the leaders of my country, for the present I lay aside all thoughts of revenge; but when you resume your sword, I will go five hundred miles to demand satisfaction at the point of it, for the murder of my son." The probability is that Mrs. McKay used no such stately language. No doubt she walked up to Brown, shook her finger in his face, and exclaimed, "You miserable villain! I can't get at you now; but if the day ever comes, I'll flay you alive for the murder of my poor boy."

The fall of Augusta was received with rejoicings by
the patriots everywhere, and the British and the Tories
were correspondingly depressed. Men who had been
overawed by the cruelty of the Tories, now came out
boldly for the cause of independence, and the forces
of the Americans were rapidly strengthened. Preparations were made for an aggressive campaign in Georgia
by the Liberty Boys; and in this purpose they had the
active aid and sympathy of General Greene, whose skill
and ability as a commander were not greater than the
wisdom he displayed in dealing with the people.

In January, 1782, General Greene ordered General
Anthony Wayne to take charge of the campaign in
Georgia. At the same time he wrote a letter to Governor Martin that displays better than any document
now extant the sagacity and conservatism that were the
basis of General Greene's character and the source of
his great success as a commander. "I cannot help
recommending to your Excellency," he wrote to the
governor of Georgia, "to open a door for the disaffected
in your State to come in, with particular exceptions. It
is better to save than to destroy, especially when we
are obliged to expose good men to destroy bad. It is
always dangerous to push people to a state of desperation; and the satisfaction of revenge has but a momentary existence, and is commonly succeeded by pity and
remorse. The practice of plundering, which, I am told,
has been too much indulged with you, is very destructive to the morals and manners of the people. Habits
and dispositions founded on this practice soon grow
obstinate, and are difficult to restrain; indeed, it is the

most direct way of undermining all government, and never fails to bring the laws into contempt, for people will not stop at the barriers which were first intended to bound them after having tasted the sweets of possessing property by the easy mode of plunder. The preservation of morals and an encouragement to honest industry should be the first objects of government. Plundering is the destruction of both. I wish the cause of liberty may never be tarnished with inhumanity, nor the morals of people bartered in exchange for wealth."

This letter was intended to put an end to the war of extermination that the Tories of Upper Georgia had begun, and to prevent the patriots from carrying out their plans of revenge. The letter did great good. It was turned over to the Legislature by the governor, and thus made public; and its sentiments were taken to heart by hundreds who had suffered the most cruel wrongs at the hands of the Tories. General Greene's letter was also made the basis of two proclamations, both issued by the governor after conference with General Wayne. One opened the door to disaffected Georgians who might desire to return to the ranks of the republicans, and the other was addressed to the Hessian troops who had already begun to sympathize with the Salzburghers at Ebenezer. Stevens, in his "History of Georgia," says that many citizens who had been compelled from various reasons to seek protection under the British Government, and who had even joined the armies of the enemy, took advantage of the proclamation which referred to them, returned to their State allegiance, and joined the forces of General

STO. OF GA. — 8

Wayne, where they proved their sincerity by making the most zealous efforts to merit the pardon and protection that had been promised them by the governor.

After a brilliant campaign, lasting from January to July, 1782, General Wayne, assisted by Elijah Clarke, James Jackson, and other bold spirits who had never suffered the fires of liberty to go out in Georgia, cleared the State of the British. Savannah was occupied on the 11th of July, the keys having been surrendered to James Jackson. This was the end of British rule in Georgia.

A NEGRO PATRIOT.

ALONG with the emigrants from North Carolina who first settled Wilkes County, there came a man named Aycock. He brought with him a mulatto boy named Austin. This boy passed as Aycock's slave; but when the conflict between the Liberty Boys and the Tories in that part of the country became desperate, — when the patriots were fighting for their lives as well as for the liberties of their country, — Aycock's neighbors called on him to do his part. According to all accounts, Aycock was not much of a warrior. His sympathies were with his liberty-loving neighbors; but his enthusiasm did not invite him to expose himself to the fire of musketry. It is said that he joined the neighbors, and strove to be a faithful militiaman, but he was in a state of constant fear. Governor Gilmer says of Aycock, that, from the time he was required to fight, he saw a terrible Tory constantly pointing a loaded gun at him. His alarm finally became so extreme that he offered as his substitute the mulatto boy Austin, who had then grown to be a stout and serviceable lad.

Objection was made that Austin was a slave, and could not therefore be received as a soldier. At this, Aycock acknowledged that Austin was no slave; that, although he was a mulatto, he had been born free. This fact was made so clear to the patriots, that they willingly received Austin as a soldier, and he was mustered into the service under the name of Austin Dabney. He fought under Elijah Clarke, being under the command of Colonel John Dooly, who was afterwards so foully murdered by the Tories. Of all the brave men that fought under the heroic Clarke, there was none braver than Austin Dabney, none that did better service.

He was in the battle of Kettle Creek, and was foremost among those who followed Clarke. Toward the close of this the bloodiest battle fought in Georgia between the patriots and Tories, Austin Dabney was shot through the thigh, and so dangerously wounded that he became a cripple for life. He was taken by his comrades to the house of a Mr. Harris, where he was carefully nursed until his wound healed. He was not able to do military duty after that, but he devoted himself to Harris and his family more faithfully than any slave could have done. It may be said of him that gratitude became the ruling passion of his heart.

After the Americans had won their independence, and peace with it, Austin Dabney became prosperous.

Being a quick-witted man, with an instinct for business, he accumulated property. He finally moved to Madison County, taking with him his benefactor and family, to whose wants and desires he continued to minister with as much devotion as he displayed at the beginning of his service. It was in Madison County that Austin Dabney became noted for his fondness for horse-racing. He attended all the races in the neighboring counties. He was the owner of some of the finest race horses to be found in the country; and such was his popularity, that he always found prominent men to stand for him.

Shortly after he removed to Madison County, he received a pension from the United States Government. He sent Harris's oldest son to school, and afterwards to college. When the young man graduated from Franklin College, now the State University, Austin Dabney supported him while he studied law with Hon. Stephen Upson at Lexington, Oglethorpe County. When young Harris was undergoing his examination for admission to the bar, Austin Dabney stood leaning against the railing that inclosed the court, listening to the proceedings with great anxiety. When the young man was sworn in, and was shaking hands with the members of the bar, Austin, unable to control himself, burst into a flood of tears, happy that he had been able to make a gentleman of the son of the man who had nursed him so long and patiently while his wound was healing.

When the public lands in Georgia were distributed among the people by lottery, the Legislature gave to Austin Dabney a lot of land in Walton County. The next year the voters of Madison County were in a condition bordering on distraction, being divided into Dabney and anti-Dabney parties. Austin had not been permitted to have a chance in the lottery with other soldiers of the Revolution. Consequently Stephen Upson, one of Georgia's most prominent men at that time, employed his influence with such effect that a law was passed giving Dabney a valuable lot. One of the members of the Legislature from Madison County voted for this law. At the next election the constituents of this member divided themselves into two parties, one faction indorsing the vote, and the other denouncing it. Those who denounced the vote did it on the ground that it was an indignity to white men for a mulatto to be put on an equality with them in the distribution of the public land, though, as Governor Gilmer bluntly puts it, not one of them had served his country so long or so well.

Governor Gilmer, from whose writings all facts about Austin Dabney are taken, tells a very interesting anecdote about him. In order to collect the pension which the United States Government allowed on account of his broken thigh, Austin went once a year to Savannah. Once when he was on his way to draw what was due him, he fell in with Colonel Wiley Pope, his neighbor, who was also journeying to Savannah. They were very intimate and social on the road, and until they found themselves in the streets of Savannah. When they reached the fashionable part of the city, Colonel Pope observed to his companion that he was a sensible man, and knew the prejudices that prevented them from associating together in the city. Austin Dabney replied that he understood it very well, and with that he checked his horse and fell in the rear of Colonel Pope after the fashion of a servant following his master. Their way led them in front of the house of General James Jackson, who was at that time governor of the State. The governor was standing in his door at the time. Colonel Pope passed on unrecognized, but, chancing to glance around, he saw Governor Jackson run from the house into the street to greet Austin Dabney. The governor seized the negro's hand, shook it heartily, drew him from his horse, and carried him into the house, where he remained a welcome guest during his stay in the city. Colonel Pope (so Governor Gilmer says) used to tell this story with great glee, but owned that he felt put out when he realized, that, whilst he was a stranger at a tavern, Austin Dabney was the honored guest of the governor of the State. The explanation was, that Governor Jackson had seen Dabney's courage and patriotism tested on the field of battle, and he knew that beneath the tawny skin of the mulatto there beat the heart of a true man.

Austin Dabney was always popular with those who knew of his services in the Revolutionary War. Governor Gilmer says that he was one of the best chroniclers of the stirring events of that period. His memory was retentive, his understanding good, and he had a gift of description possessed by few. He moved to the land the State had given him, taking with him the family of the man who had nursed him. He continued to serve them while he lived, faithful to the end, and when he died left them the property he had accumulated.

THE YAZOO FRAUD.

SOME writers on the early history of Georgia have been under the impression that the speculation known as the Yazoo Fraud had its beginning in the efforts of General Elijah Clarke and his followers to settle on the Indian reservation lying west of the Oconee River; but this is not the case at all. General Clarke's movement was the result of an enterprise which was aimed against the Spaniards; and, though the facts have no real connection with the Yazoo speculation, they may be briefly told here, especially since Stevens, in his "History of Georgia," turns them all topsy-turvy.

Genet was the first envoy sent to represent the wild and revolutionary republic of France, — the republic of Robespierre and the Jacobins. He represented, as well as any man could, the ideas and purposes of those who had wrought such havoc in France. He was meddle-some, wrong-headed, unreasonable, and bold with it all. He sailed from France in a ship which he commanded himself; and instead of going straight to Philadelphia (then the seat of government), where his business called him, he landed at Charleston in South Carolina. War was then pending between France and Spain; and Genet, after landing in Charleston, found ready sym-pathizers in the French Huguenots of South Carolina, and indeed in all those who had fought for American liberty. There were two reasons why the fiery appeals of Genet to the people of Carolina to take up arms against Spain were received enthusiastically. One was, that the Spaniards in Florida had been at constant war with the people of Georgia and Carolina, and had committed many crimes and depredations. The other was, that the people felt grateful to France for the aid she had given the American Colonies in their efforts to shake off the yoke of Great Britain.

Genet's plan was to raise in this country an army large enough to seize the Spanish possessions in Florida, and to reconquer Louisiana. For the reasons stated, Genet found the people enthusiastic in favor of his enterprise. The enthusiasm was intense. It crossed the Savannah, and found General Elijah Clarke, with his strong nature and active sympathies, ready to embrace it. His military prestige in the South commended him to Genet as the man to lead the military enterprise against the Spanish settlements in the South. Accordingly he was given command of the army that was to be raised, and was made a major general in the French service with a pay of ten thousand dollars.

Having secured a commander whose courage and resources in the field could be depended on, Genet went from Charleston to Philadelphia overland, stirring up sympathy for his enterprise and enlisting men. His success was greater than he had dreamed of. He found but one thing in his way, and that was the firmness and vigilance of George Washington. This great man set his face sternly against the project; but such was the enthusiasm of the people, — artfully stirred by Genet, who was as accomplished as he was unscrupulous, — that a French party was formed. Genet took advantage of the formation of this party to arouse prejudice against Washington; and such was his success, that John Adams, who was afterwards President, says that there was a multitude of men in Philadelphia ready to drive Washington from the executive chair.

A considerable army was raised, recruits reported to General Clarke from the Ohio River to the St. Mary's, and everything was ready for action. At that moment the heavy hand of Washington descended on the enterprise. The recall of Genet was demanded, the French party went to pieces, the project collapsed, and Elijah Clarke was left without resources, surrounded by a considerable force of men who had come at his bidding to take part in the attack on the Spanish possessions. These men were on his hands, expecting the fulfillment of promises that had been made to them. What was to be done? It was at this critical period that the eyes of General Clarke turned to the Indian reservation west of the Oconee. He marched his men to these lands, and took possession. He, and those who engaged in the movement for settling the lands, had risked their lives for their country on a hundred battlefields. They thought that the lands that had been claimed by the King belonged to those who had conquered the King's armies. They were right in principle, but wrong in action. The lands that had belonged to the King now belonged to the people, not as individuals, but as a corporate body, — to the whole people represented by the

State government. These principles had not been made as clear by discussion in General Clarke's day as they have been made since. He engaged in no speculation. He boldly settled the lands, and was prepared to boldly hold his position. The settlement was made in 1794. On the 28th of July, Governor George Matthews issued a proclamation forbidding the settlement, and likewise directed one of the judges to issue a warrant for the general's arrest. At the Superior Court of Wilkes County, Clarke surrendered himself to the judge, who referred the case to the county justices. These judges made a decision, setting forth the fact that Elijah Clarke had surrendered himself into custody; that, being desirous to do speedy justice to the State as well as to the party charged, they had proceeded to maturely consider the case; and that after examining the laws of the State, and the treaties made and laws passed by the United States, they gave it as their "decided and unanimous opinion that the said Elijah Clarke be and is hereby discharged." Encouraged by this decision, General Clarke returned to his settlement with the intention of holding the lands; but finally both the Federal and the State governments moved against him, and he abandoned the enterprise. The policy that Clarke began in settling the Indian lands without regard to the rights of the savage has since become the policy of the government. It is not a wholesome policy, nor is it authorized by the moral or civil law; but it has been unblushingly carried out nevertheless.

The Yazoo Fraud was a far different matter. The very name of it was foreign to Georgia. It was borrowed from the Indian name of a small stream which empties itself into the Mississippi River. When the Colony of Georgia was first settled, the land granted to Oglethorpe was described as lying along the Savannah River, extending southward along the coast to the Altamaha, and from the head waters of these rivers westward to "the South Seas." Afterwards Great Britain changed the line which he had established. She carried the boundary line of West Florida, a part of her possessions, higher up. The new line started from the Mississippi at the mouth of the Yazoo River, and ran due east to the Chattahoochee at a point near where the town of West Point now stands. As the upper boundary of British West Florida this line came to be known as the Yazoo line, and the country above and below it to an indefinite extent came to be known as the Yazoo country. No boundary can now be fixed to the region then known as the Yazoo country. At the close of the Revolutionary War, Great Britain made a treaty which has been interpreted as vesting in the United States and in Georgia the right and title to these lands, reaching from the Chattahoochee to the Yazoo River, and extending on each side of this line to a distance that has never been estimated.

The Yazoo Fraud itself had a somewhat vague beginning. From the best information that can now be obtained, it may be said that it was set on foot in 1789, shortly after the close of the Revolution, by a sharper who was famous in that day. He was known as Thomas Washington, but his real name was Walsh. Washington, or Walsh, is described as being a very extraordinary man. He had fought in the service of Georgia, but he had the instinct of a speculator; and when the war was ended, he gave himself up to the devices of those who earn their living by their wits. He was a man of good address, and his air of candor succeeded in deceiving all whom he met. Those who dealt with him always had the worst of the bargain.

When Washington, or Walsh, began to operate in Georgia through agents, he found the way already prepared for him. The War for Independence had barely closed, when certain individuals, most of them men of some influence, began to look on our Western possessions with a greedy eye. They had an idea of securing these lands and setting up a new government, — a sort of Western empire. To further their designs they began by forming themselves into an association called the "Combined Society," the members of which were bound to secrecy by oaths and other solemn pledges. The purpose of the Combined Society became known, and the force of public opinion compelled the members to disband. Some of them were men of aristocratic pretensions.

Thus Washington, or Walsh, found a great many sympathetic people in Georgia. He was too well known in the State to undertake any scheme to which his name was attached: so he worked through an agent, a man named Sullivan. This man Sullivan had been a captain in the patriot army; but he had headed the Philadelphia mob which insulted Congress, and he was compelled to flee to the Mississippi to save his neck. When the old Congress went out, Sullivan felt free to

return. He came to Georgia, representing, or pretending to represent, the Virginia Yazoo Company, of
which the celebrated Patrick Henry was a member,
and made application to the State Legislature for the
purchase of the Western lands. Sullivan's description
of the Yazoo lands was so glowing that another company was formed in Georgia. Some of the members of
the new company formerly belonged to the Combined
Society, but others were men of good standing. This
company employed active agents ; but no corrupt means
were used so far as is now known, though some members of the General Assembly were interested. The
efforts of the company were successful. Their act was
passed, and ·the sale made. Immediately the people
began to oppose the scheme, and to demand the repeal
of the act. The demand grew into a State issue, and the
new Legislature declared the sale null and void.

For a while the land grabbers were quiet ; but in 1794
it seemed to the most eager of the speculators that the
time had come for them to make another effort to
secure the rich Western lands that belonged to the State.
They were evidently afraid, that, unless they made
haste to get hold of the lands, the people's Legislature
would divide them out or sell them to the Federal
Government. So they formed another conspiracy, and
this time they laid their plans very deep. Acting on
the principle that every man has his price, they
managed, by bribery and other underhanded schemes,
to win the sympathy and support of some of the most
prominent men in the State, — men whose names
seemed to be far above suspicion. Some of the highest

judges lent their aid to the land grabbers. Members of Congress were concerned in the scheme. Generals and other high officers of the militia took part in it. Nothing was left undone that was calculated to win the support of men who, up to that time, had enjoyed and deserved the confidence and respect of the State. The extent of the bribery and corruption that existed would be altogether beyond belief if the records were not left to show it.

The swindlers were both bold and cunning, and in one way or another sought to win the support of all the leading men of the State. And they came very near succeeding.

The Legislature held its session in Augusta at that time; and while the Yazoo land sale was up for discussion, the agents of the land grabbers swarmed around it, coaxing, bribing, and bullying the people's representatives. Among these agents was a judge of the Supreme Court of the United States, from Pennsylvania, with twenty-five thousand dollars in his hands. There was a judge of the United States District Court for Georgia, paying shares in the land company for the votes of members. A United States senator from Georgia, James Gunn, who had neglected to return to his post of duty in Congress, was seen bullying members with a loaded whip, to secure their support for the land-sale scheme. A judge of the State courts was also present, with other prominent citizens, buttonholing the members of the Legislature, offering them shares, sub-shares, and half sub-shares to secure their votes. General James Jackson, who was then a United States senator from Georgia, was told by a prominent judge of the State that he might have any number of acres he pleased up to half a million, without the payment of a dollar, if he would use his influence in behalf of the corrupt schemes of the land grabbers. In reply, General Jackson said he had fought for the people of Georgia; that the land belonged to them and to their children; and that, should the conspirators succeed, he, for one, would hold the sale to be void. Many weak men in the Legislature were intimidated by threats; and some who could not be persuaded to vote for the sale, were paid to go home, and remain away from the Legislature.

In this way the representatives of the people were persuaded and bribed to support the scheme of the land grabbers. In 1795 the bill was passed, selling to four companies — the Georgia Company, the Georgia Mississippi Company, the Upper Mississippi Company, and the Tennessee Company — thirty-five million acres of land for $500,000. Nothing was now wanting to complete the fraud but the signature of the governor. If he put his name to the bill, it became a law. If he refused to sign it, the scheme of the swindlers would fail. General George Matthews was the governor at that time, and, though two of his sons had been made members of the land-grabbing companies, it was hoped that he would refuse to sign the bill. The hope was justified by the fact that he had refused to sign a similar bill, and had given some very good reasons for it. It was known, too, that he was a man of great courage, and honest in his intentions; but the influence brought to bear on him was too great. His judgment was weakened by the clamor of the prominent men around him, who had become the paid agents of the swindlers. He resisted for some time, but finally agreed to sign the bill. The secretary of Governor Matthews, a man named Urquhart, tried to prevent the signing of the bill by working on the governor's superstitions. He dipped the pen in oil, thinking that when Matthews came to write with it, and found that the ink refused to flow, he would take it as an omen that the bill should not be signed. The governor was startled, when, after several efforts, he found the pen would not write; but he was not a man to let so trifling a matter stand in his way. He directed his secretary to make another pen, and with this he made the land-steal bill a law. By a stroke he made the bill a law, and also signed away his own popularity and influence. The people of Georgia never trusted him afterwards; and he left the State, finding it unpleasant and uncomfortable to live among those who had lost

STO. OF GA. — 9

their respect for him. Yet no charge of corruption was ever made against him.

When the people learned that the Yazoo Fraud had become a law, they rose up as one man to denounce it. Those who lived in the neighborhood of Augusta determined to put to death the men who had betrayed them. They marched to the legislative halls, and were only prevented from carrying out their threats by the persuasion of the small minority of the members that had refused to be coaxed, bullied, or bribed into voting for the Yazoo Fraud. But the indignation of the people continued to grow as they learned of the corrupt methods that had been employed to pass the measure. Meetings were held in every county; and public opinion became so strong that those who had voted for the Yazoo Fraud found it dangerous to remain in the State. A senator from Hancock County became so alarmed that he fled to South Carolina. He was followed by one of his neighbors, found in a lonely cabin at night, and shot to death. Except in one or two counties, the men who voted for the Yazoo Fraud were compelled to hide themselves until the anger of the people had cooled.

In his "Sketches of the First Settlers of Upper Georgia," Governor George R. Gilmer tells a little story that will serve to show the state of feeling in Georgia at that time. After the Yazoo Fraud was passed, the people of the counties held indignation meetings. A meeting was called in Oglethorpe County, and on the morning of the day, a citizen on his way to town stopped at the gate of a neighbor to wait until he could get ready to go. The man who was getting ready was named Miles Jennings. The citizen, waiting, saw Mr. Jennings put a rope in his pocket.

"What is that for?" the citizen asked.

"To hang Musgrove!" replied Mr. Jennings, Musgrove being the name of the member of the Legislature.

When the two neighbors arrived at the courthouse, all the people had assembled. Mr. Jennings hitched his horse, went into the crowd, pulled the rope from his pocket, and, holding it above his head where all could see it, cried out, —

"Neighbors! this rope is to hang Musgrove, who sold the people's land for a bribe!"

The words of Jennings and the sight of the rope made the people furious. Musgrove had been given a hint by Jennings's neighbor, and he had made good his escape. But for that, no human power could have saved him.

The whole State was in a condition of excitement that is hard to describe. Grand juries made presentments, county and town meetings passed resolutions, and petitions were sent from hand to hand, and signed by hundreds of people. A State convention, called to alter the constitution, had been chosen to meet in May, 1795, but the members had been chosen at the same time that the members of the corrupt Legislature had been elected; and a majority of them had been "tarred with the same stick," as the saying goes. The present-ments, resolutions, and petitions crowded so fast upon the convention, that it was decided to postpone the changing of the constitution to a time when the people were in a better humor. The convention referred all the papers it had received to the next Legislature, and adjourned in some confusion.

This added to the excitement and anger of the peo-ple. They were in doubt how to act. Delay would give the land grabbers time to sell the lands they had secured through bribery and corruption. But whom could the people trust? They had been betrayed by many of their highest judges, by one of their United States senators, and by a large majority of their Legis-lature. A great many believed that all the powers of government had come to an end.

During the troubled times of the Revolution it had been the custom of military officers having the confi-dence of the people to convene the Legislative Assembly when an emergency seemed to call for it. In the midst of their doubt and confusion, the people applied to Gen-eral Twiggs, the senior major general, to convene the Legislature in order that action might be taken before the swindlers sold the lands they had obtained by fraud; but General Twiggs refused to act in a case in which he had no clear right and power, so the people remained for the time being without a remedy.

From the very beginning of this scheme to defraud the people of the State, it had been bitterly opposed by General James Jackson, who was representing Georgia in the United States Senate. He denounced it in the Senate. He corresponded with the most eminent men in the State, he wrote to the newspapers, and in every possible way held up to the scorn and contempt of the public the men who were trying to defraud the State of its rich Western lands. On the other hand, the conspirators left nothing undone to injure the reputation of General Jackson. His character was attacked, and his life was several times threatened. As early as the spring of 1795, he took occasion in full Senate, and in the presence of General James Gunn (the Georgia senator who was representing the swindlers), to denounce the scheme as "a speculation of the darkest character and of deliberate villany."

By his bold, even violent opposition to the Yazoo sale, General Jackson had made himself the leader of the people. Therefore in 1795, while he was still senator, many of the people requested him to resign, so that he might use his influence and great talents in bringing about the repeal of the obnoxious law. He tendered his resignation at once, and returned home. He was elected a member of the Legislature, and devoted all his time and all his energy to blotting out the odious law. He became a member of the committee appointed to investigate the means used to pass the law, and under his leadership the whole scandalous affair was probed to the bottom.

In electing the new Legislature, the only issue was

Yazoo and anti-Yazoo. The people were successful in
electing men who favored the repeal of the law. There
was no other business before the General Assembly
until this matter was disposed of. The body was
flooded with the petitions and remonstrances that had
been sent to the convention. The Legislature had met
in January, 1795. At once a day was set to "consider
the state of the Republic." On that day the petitions
and presentments were considered, and referred to a
committee, of which General Jackson was appointed
chairman. On the 22d of January the committee reported not only that the act was unconstitutional, but
that fraud had been practiced to secure its passage. On
these grounds they declared that the act was a nullity,
and not binding on the people of the State.

The bill declaring the sale void was drawn up by
General Jackson. It passed both Houses by large
majorities, and was signed by Governor Irwin. The
feeling of the Legislature was so strong, that, after the
Yazoo act had been repealed, it was decided to destroy
all the records and documents relating to the corruption.
By order of the two Houses a fire was kindled in the
public square of Louisville, which was then the capital.
The enrolled act that had been secured by fraud was
brought out by the secretary of state, and by him delivered to the President of the Senate for examination.
That officer delivered the act to the Speaker of the
House. The Speaker in turn passed it to the clerk,
who read the title of the act and the other records, and
then, committing them to the flames, cried out in a loud
voice, "God save the State and preserve her rights, and

may every attempt to injure them perish as these wicked and corrupt acts now do!"

The flames in which the records were burned were kindled by means of a sun glass, so that it might be truly said that fire came down from heaven to destroy the evidences of corruption. There is a tradition that when the officers of the State had met to destroy the records, an old man, a stranger to all present, rode through the multitude, and made his way to where the officials stood. Lifting up his voice, he declared, that, feeble as he was, he had come there to see an act of justice performed, but he thought the fire in which the records of corruption were to be destroyed should come from heaven. The people watched him in silence. He drew from his bosom with trembling hands a sun glass, and in this way burned the papers. Then, says tradition, the white-haired old man mounted his horse and rode away, and was never seen again.

IN giving the history of the Yazoo Fraud, mention
has been made of General George Matthews, who
was governor at the time, and who was compelled to
leave the State because he had been persuaded to sign
the bill.   General Matthews was one of the most
remarkable characters of his time.   Governor Gilmer
has drawn a very interesting portrait of him.   It is not
a pleasing picture in some respects, but it gives a very

interesting glimpse of a man who in his day was one
of the strongest characters in the State.

He was the son of an Irishman named John
Matthews, who settled in western Virginia in 1737.
George Matthews began to fight the Indians at an age
when most boys are at school. In 1761 the Indians
attacked and murdered a family not far from his
father's home. He heard the guns, and thought that
a shooting match was going on. With some companions of his own age, he rode forward to join in the
sport; but the youngsters saw the dead bodies of their
neighbors lying in the yard where they had been left
by the murderous savages, and at once turned their
horses' heads and fled. They were not a moment too
soon; for the Indians, who had been lying in ambush,
rose and fired at the boys. Matthews had a narrow
escape; for a bullet cut off the wisp of hair (known as
a queue) that hung dangling from the back of his head.
The danger that he had passed through, and the sight
of his murdered neighbors, roused young Matthews to
action. He collected a party of men, put himself at
the head of them, followed and overtook the savages,
and killed nine of their number.

In the greatest battle that ever took place between
the Virginians and the Indians, Matthews commanded
a company, and bore a very conspicuous part. The
battle took place at the junction of the Ohio River with
the Kanawha, on what was called Point Pleasant. The
fight began at sunrise, and was kept up all day, with no
great success on either side. The Indians held their
ground, and refused to give way before the most

stubborn attacks of the Virginians. Near sundown, Matthews, with two other captains, made a strategic movement. The three companies were withdrawn from the battle. Out of sight of the enemy, they got into the bed of a creek. Hidden by the banks of the stream, they marched to the rear of the Indians, and from this point made an attack. The movement had been so cleverly carried out, that the savages were taken completely by surprise, and driven across the Ohio.

Early in the Revolutionary War, General Washington, who knew well the value of the training Matthews had received on the frontier, ordered him and the regiment which he commanded to join the main army. He took part in the battle of the Brandywine; and at the battle of Germantown he led his regiment against the British opposing him, drove them back, and pushed on to the center of the town, where he captured a regiment of the enemy. Shortly after this, while engaged in a skirmish, his courage led him too close to the British. He was knocked down, severely wounded by a bayonet thrust, and taken prisoner. He was sent to the British prison ship in New York Harbor. He was there treated with so much cruelty that he appealed to his government for relief. In response to that appeal, Thomas Jefferson, who was then governor of Virginia, wrote him a personal letter, in which he said, "We know that the ardent spirit and hatred of tyranny which brought you into your present situation will enable you to bear up against it with the firmness which has distinguished you as a soldier, and look forward with pleasure to the day when events shall take place against which the wounded spirit of your enemies will find no comfort, even from reflections on the most refined of the cruelties with which they have glutted themselves."

General Matthews was not exchanged until the close of the war. He then joined the Southern army under General Greene, and commanded the Third Virginia Regiment. While in the South, he bought a tract of land on Broad River, known as the Goose Pond. He settled there with his family in 1784. The fame he had won as a soldier made General Matthews at that time the principal man in Georgia. He was elected governor in 1786. When his term expired, he was sent to Congress. In 1794–95 he was again made governor; and it was at this time, that, contrary to all expectations, he was prevailed on to sign the Yazoo Act. No charge of corruption was ever made against him. No thief or swindler was ever bold enough to try to bribe such a high-spirited and fearless man. But excitement in the State ran so high, that General Matthews was ruined so far as his influence was concerned. He left Georgia, and never afterwards made the State his home for any long period.

In 1811 a lot of runaway negroes, ruffians, and lawless men congregated in Florida in such numbers that they were able to get control of affairs. They formed a government of their own, and then petitioned the United States to make Florida one of their territories. President Madison appointed General Matthews the agent of the United States to negotiate with the "constituted authorities" for the annexation of

Florida. General Matthews made a treaty with those who were in control of Florida; but Spain protested, and the President finally declared that the treaty had not been made with the "constituted authorities."

General Matthews was not a learned man (he knew nothing of books), and he could not understand the fuss that was made over the term "constituted authorities." He became very angry with the President, said that that officer had a cowardly fear of Spain and Great Britain, and declared that he would go to Washington to "thrash" the President. He actually set out on that errand; but the fatigue and exposure which he had experienced in Florida, and the high state of excitement under which he labored, threw him into a fever while he was on his journey to Washington, and he died in Augusta in March, 1812.

Previous to his Florida appointment, General Matthews had been nominated to be governor of the Territory of Mississippi by President Adams; but the opposition was so great that the President withdrew the nomination. When General Matthews heard of this, he promptly set out for Philadelphia to call the President to account. He rode to Mr. Adams's house, gave a loud knock on the door, and told the servant he wished to see the President. The servant said the President was engaged; but General Matthews bristled with anger at the bare thought that any man, even the President, could be engaged in any business more important than talking to George Matthews, late colonel of the Virginia line, and governor of the State of Georgia. Therefore he told the servant to go at once and tell the President that a gentleman wished to speak to him; and he added, that, if the message was not carried at once, the servant would find his head taken from his shoulders. General Matthews wore his Revolutionary sword and cocked hat, and he succeeded in convincing the servant that he was not to be trifled with. He was promptly admitted into the presence of Mr. Adams, and, with the touch of Irish brogue he had caught from his father, he made himself and his business known. He introduced himself, and then said to the President, —

" Now, sir, I understand that you nominated me to the Senate of these United States, to be governor of the Territory of Mississippi, and that afterwards you took back the nomination. Sir, if you had known me, you would not have taken the nomination back. If you did not know me, you should not have nominated me to so important an office. Now, sir, unless you can satisfy me, your station as President of these United States shall not screen you from my vengeance."

Mr. Adams at once made himself agreeable, for he had nothing but good will for the stanch Georgia Federalist. The outcome of the meeting was that the President promised to appoint the general's son John to be supervisor of the revenue, and this promise he carried out.

Governor Gilmer, in his racy reminiscences of the people who settled in the Broad River region, draws an interesting portrait of General Matthews. He describes him as a short, thick man, with stout legs, on which he stood very straight. "He carried his head rather thrown back. His features were full and bluff, his hair light red, and his complexion fair and florid. He admitted no superior but General Washington. He spoke of his services to his country as unsurpassed except by those of his great chief. He wore a three-cornered cocked hat, top boots, a shirt full ruffled at the bosom and wrists, and sometimes a long sword at his side. To listen to his talk about himself, his children, and his affairs, one would have thought that he was but a puff of wind. Trade or talk of history with him, and he was found to be one of the shrewdest of men. Fight with him, and he never failed to act the hero. He was unlearned. He spelled 'coffee' k-a-u-g-h-p-h-y. He wrote 'Congress' with a *K*."

When it is considered that he had small opportunity to train himself in any direction except rough fighting, General Matthews must be regarded as one of the most remarkable men of his time.

Another remarkable man who figured largely in both the military and political history of the State was General John Clarke, son of the famous Elijah Clarke. John Clarke became a soldier in the Revolutionary War when a mere boy. He had followed his father to camp, and remained with him. He took part in many skirmishes; but at the battle of Kettle Creek, in Wilkes County, he distinguished himself by his coolness and courage. He fought through the war. He was made a lieutenant at sixteen years of age, and when the war ended he was a major. After the war he was made a brigadier, and then a major general of the militia. After aiding to run the British out of the State, and subduing the Tories, General Clarke turned his attention to the Indians. At the battle of Jacks Creek, in Walton County, in 1787, he greatly distinguished himself, having charge of one of the wings of the Georgia forces.

It was natural that a man raised in camp, and brought up in the midst of the rough and tough elements that are collected together there, should possess qualities not calculated to fit him for the polite transactions that take place in drawing rooms and parlors. General Clarke's self-reliance was extreme. Having commanded men from the time he was sixteen, it was natural that his temper and his manners should be offensive, to some extent, to those who were not thoughtful enough to make due allowance for these things. It thus happened that when peace came, John Clarke's methods and practices made him many bitter enemies. On the other hand, the sterling qualities of his character made him many strong friends.

Coming out of the war with neither trade nor profession, and with only the rudiments of an education, John Clarke was compelled to turn his attention to politics. With him politics was simply a modified form of war. He had never given any quarter to the Tories, and he gave small quarter to his political enemies. But he was as faithful to his friends in politics as he had been to the cause of American liberty. He was uncompromising, whether dealing with friends or enemies, and his temper was such that he regarded his opponents as his personal enemies. Of his political career, mention will be made in another place. It is sufficient to say that a quarrel he had with a judge divided the people of the State into two parties, and the contest between them was carried on for several years. The prejudices that sprang up in that contest lasted for more than a generation, and strong traces of them are to be found in estimates of General Clarke's character written long after he was dead.

Only a man of the strongest character, and possessing the most remarkable qualities, could have made such a marked impression on the political history of a commonwealth.

AFTER THE REVOLUTION.

THE Revolution came to an end in Georgia when, on the 11th of July, *1782*, Savannah was taken possession of by the American troops under General Anthony Wayne. It ended for the whole country when, on the 30th of November of the same year, the treaty of peace was signed at Paris between the United States and Great Britain. The King of Great Britain acknowledged the independence of the Thirteen States, and declared them free and sovereign. This was a very happy event for the country, and had been long looked forward to by the people, sometimes doubtfully, but always hopefully.

But the great victory that had been won found the people of Georgia prostrate. The little property that they possessed when the war began had either been spent in maintaining the struggle, or well-nigh destroyed by the raids of the British and Tories. In the larger communities of Savannah and Augusta, the citizens had the resources of trade and commerce to fall back on, but in the smaller settlements and rural districts the condition of the inhabitants bordered on destitution.

At the time that Savannah was surrendered to the American troops, there was almost a famine in the land. The soldiers were without shoes, and sometimes they were without supplies. The crops were short on account of the lack of farmers. The condition of the people was quite as bad as that of the troops, especially when the disbanded militia returned to their homes. Houses, barns, and fences had been burned; stock and cattle had been slaughtered or driven away; and there was a great lack of even the necessities of life.

But those whose energy and spirit upheld them through the long struggle for independence were not the men to surrender to the hard circumstances that surrounded them. They went to work as bravely as they had fought; and the sacrifices they made to peace were almost as severe, though not so bloody, as those they had made to war. Slowly, but surely and steadily, they reclaimed their waste farms. Slowly, but surely and steadily, they recovered from the prostration that the war had brought on their industries. Slowly, but surely and steadily, the people worked their way back to comparative prosperity. There may have been a few drones in the towns, but there were no idle hands in the country places.

The men built for their families comfortable log

cabins; and these, with their clean sanded floors, are still the fashion in some parts of Georgia. This done, they went about the business of raising crops, and stocking their farms with cattle. The women and children were just as busy. In every cabin could be heard the hum of the spinning wheel, and the thump of the old hand loom. While the men were engaged in their outdoor work, the women spun, wove, and made the comfortable jeans clothes that were the fashion; while the girls plaited straw, and made hats and bonnets, and in many other ways helped the older people. In a little while peddlers from the more northern States began to travel through Georgia with their various wares, some with pewter plates and spoons, and some with clocks. The peddlers traveled in wagons instead of carrying their packs on their backs, and in this way brought a great deal of merchandise to the State.

As was natural, the political development of Georgia was much more rapid than its industrial progress. In January, 1783, Lyman Hall was elected governor. He was distinguished for the patriotic stand he took at the very beginning of the controversy between the Colony and the King. The Legislature met in Savannah after the evacuation of the town by the British; but it was so far from the central and upper portions of the State, and there was so much dissatisfaction among the people on this account, that in May Augusta was made the capital. In that town the General Assembly met July 8, 1783. Measures were at once taken to seize land, and confiscate the property of those Royalists who had lived in Georgia. This property was sold for the benefit of the public. In November of the same year a new cession of land was obtained from the Creek nation by treaty. This was divided into the counties of Franklin and Washington, and the land distributed in bounties to the soldiers of the war.

It is worthy of note that about this time, when the State had hardly begun to recover from the effects of the war, the representatives of the people began to move in the matter of education. The Constitution of 1777 had declared that "schools shall be erected in each county, and supported by the general expense of the State." On the 31st of July, 1783, the Legislature appropriated one thousand acres of land to each county for the support of free schools. In 1784, a short time after the notification of the treaty of peace, the Legislature passed an act appropriating forty thousand acres of land for the endowment of a college or university. A year later the charter for this university was granted; and the preamble of the act declares it to be the policy of the State to foster education in the most liberal way. It so happened that some of the provisions that had been made for public education were not carried out at once, and the people of the various settlements established schools of their own. Many of the best teachers of the country came to Georgia from the more northern States; and some of them won a reputation that has lasted to this day. Later, more than one of these teachers established schools that became famous all over the country. In this way the reign of the "old field schoolmaster" began, and continued for many years.

The people had been cultivating cotton on a small scale before 1791; but the staple was so difficult to handle, that the planting was limited. Those who grew it were compelled to separate the seed from

the lint by hand, and this was so tedious that few people would grow it. But in 1793, Eli Whitney, who was living on the plantation of General Greene, near Savannah, invented the cotton gin. The machine was a very awkward and cumbrous affair compared with the gins of the present day; but in that day and time, and for many years after, the Whitney was sufficient for the needs of the people. It was one of the most important inventions that have ever been made. It gave to the commerce of the world a staple commodity that is in universal demand, and it gave to the people of the South their most valuable and important crop. But for this timely invention, the cultivation of cotton would have been confined to the narrowest limits. The gin proved to be practicable, and it came into use very quickly. The farmers prospered, and gradually increased the cotton crop.

The population also increased very rapidly. The rich lands were purchased and settled on by farmers from Virginia and the Carolinas. The colony that had been planted by Oglethorpe had never ventured very far from the seacoast. A few probably followed the course of the Savannah River, and made their homes in that region; but the people brought over by Oglethorpe were not of the stuff that pioneers are made of. The experience they had undergone in the mother country had tamed them to such a degree that they had no desire to brave the future in the wilderness. Adventures of that kind were left for the hardy North Carolinians and Virginians who first settled what was then known as Upper Georgia. After the Revolution, this tide of immigration increased very rapidly, and it was still further swelled by the profits that the Whitney gin enabled the planters of Georgia to make out of their cotton crops.

The settling of Georgia began with the charitable scheme of Oglethorpe. The making of Georgia began when the North Carolinians and Virginians began to

open up the Broad River region to the north of
Augusta. It was due to the desperate stand taken by
these hardy pioneers that Georgia continued the struggle for American independence. To Upper Georgia
came some of the best families from Virginia and North
Carolina,—the Grattons, the Lewises, the .Clarkes, the
Strothers, the Crawfords, the Reeses, the Harrises,
the Andrewses, the Taliaferros (pronounced Tollivers),
the Campbells, the Barnetts, the Toombses, the Doolys,
and many other families whose names have figured in
the history of the country. Here also settled James
Jack, the sturdy patriot who volunteered to carry the
Mecklenburg Declaration of Independence to Philadelphia. The Congress then in session chose to shut its
eyes to that declaration, but it was the basis and
framework of the Declaration afterwards written by
Thomas Jefferson.

After the Revolution, when the Cherokees went on
the warpath, the Virginia settlement was in a state of
great alarm. Men, women, and children met together,
and decided that it would be safer to camp in the woods
in a body at night rather than run the risk of being
burned to death in houses that they could not defend.
They went into the depths of the woods and made an
encampment. One night while they were around a fire,
cooking their supper, suddenly the report of a gun was
heard, and then there was a cry of " Indians!" The
men seized their guns; but they hardly knew where to
turn, or what to do. Suddenly a lad who had not lost his
head emptied a bucket of water on the fire. This was
the thing to do, but no one else had thought of it. The

name of the lad was Meriwether Lewis. He went into the regular army, became the private secretary of President Jefferson, and was selected to head the party that explored the Territory of Louisiana, which had been bought from France. Meriwether Lewis selected for his companion Captain Clark, an old army friend and comrade. Leading the party, Lewis and his friend Clark left St. Louis, and pushed westward to the Pacific coast, through dangers and obstacles that few men would have cared to meet. The famous expedition of Lewis and Clark has now become a part of the history of the country. Lewis took possession of the Pacific coast in the name of the United States. There was a controversy with Great Britain some years afterwards as to the title of Oregon, but that which Lewis and Clark had established was finally acknowledged to be the best.

Meriwether Lewis won a name in history because the opportunity came to him. His name is mentioned here because he was a representative of the men who settled Upper Georgia, — the men who kept the fires of liberty alive in the State, and who, after helping to conquer the British and the Tories, became the conquerors of the wilderness that lay to the west of them. From Wilkes, Burke, Elbert, and the region where Clarke and his men had fought, the tide of emigration slowly moved across the State, settling Greene, Hancock, Baldwin, Putnam, Morgan, Jasper, Butts, Monroe, Coweta, Upson, Pike, Meriwether, Talbot, Harris, and Muscogee counties.

Some of the more adventurous crossed the Chat-

tahoochee into Alabama, and on into the great Mississippi Valley and beyond. Their descendants live in
every part of the South; and Alabama, Mississippi,
and Texas have had Georgians for their governors, and
their senators and representatives in Congress, — men
who were descended from the Virginia and North Carolina immigrants. One of the most brilliant of these was
Mirabeau B. Lamar, scholar, statesman, and soldier, the
president of Texas when that Territory had declared
itself a free and an independent republic.

THE COTTON GIN.

BRIEF mention has been made of Whitney's invention of the cotton gin. The event was of such world-wide importance that the story should be told here. Whitney, the inventor of the gin, was born in Massachusetts in 1765, in very poor circumstances. While the War of the Revolution was going on, he was earning his living by making nails by hand. He was such an apt mechanic that he was able to make and save enough money to pay his way through Yale College, where he graduated in 1792. In that year he engaged himself to come to Georgia as a private tutor in the family of a gentleman of Savannah; but when he reached that city, he found that the place had been filled.

While in Savannah, Whitney attracted the attention of the widow of General Nathanael Greene, who lived at Mulberry Grove, on the river at no great distance from the city. Mrs. Greene invited the young man to make his home on her plantation. He soon found opportunity to show his fine mechanical genius, and Mrs. Greene became more interested in him than ever.

The story goes, that soon after the young man had established himself on the Mulberry Grove Plantation. several Georgia planters were dining with Mrs. Greene. During their conversation the difficulty of removing the seed from the cotton fiber was mentioned, and the suggestion was made that this might be done by machinery. At this Mrs. Greene mentioned the skill and ingenuity of young Whitney, and advised her guests that he should be given the problem to solve. This advice was followed. The planters had a talk with the young man, and explained to him the difficulty which they found in separating the seed from the lint.

At that time one pound of lint cotton was all that a negro woman could separate from the seed in a day; and the more cotton the planters raised, the deeper they got in debt. The close of the war had found them in a state of the utmost poverty, so that they had been compelled to mortgage their lands in order to get money on which to begin business. Cotton was the only product of the farm for which there was any constant demand; but, owing to the labor of separating the lint from the seed, it could not be raised at a profit. Thus, in 1791, the number of pounds exported from the South to Europe amounted to only about 379 bales of 500 pounds each.

When the planters went to Whitney with their problem, he was entirely ignorant of the whole matter. He knew nothing of cotton or of cotton planting; but he at once set himself at work. He made a careful study of the cotton plant. He shut himself in a room with some uncleaned cotton, and worked at his task during a whole winter. He made his own tools at the plantation blacksmith shop; and all day long, and sometimes far into the night, he could be heard hammering and sawing away.

In 1793 he called together the planters who had asked

him to solve the problem, and showed them the machine, which he called a cotton gin. When they saw it work, their surprise and delight knew no bounds. They knew

at once that the problem had been solved by the young genius from Massachusetts. Little calculation was needed to show them that the cotton gin could clean as much cotton in a day as could be cleaned on a plantation during a whole winter. What before had been the work of a hundred hands for several months could now be completed in a few days.

But it seems to be the fate of the majority of those who make wonderful inventions never to enjoy the full benefits of the work of their genius. Eli Whitney was not an exception to the general rule. While he was working on his cotton gin, rumors of it went abroad; and by the time it was completed, public expectation was on tiptoe. When the machine was finished, it was shown to only a few people; but the fact, of such immense importance to the people of the State, was soon known throughout the State, and the planters impatiently waited for the day when they would be able to put it in use.

One night the building in which Whitney's cotton gin was concealed was broken into, ransacked, and the machine carried off. It was a bold robbery, and a very successful one. The inventor made haste to build another gin; but before he could get his model completed, and obtain a patent right to the invention, the machine had been manufactured at various points in the South by other parties, and was in operation on several plantations. Whitney formed a partnership with a gentleman who had some capital, and went to Connecticut to manufacture his gin; but he was compelled to spend all the money he could make, fighting lawsuits. His patent had been infringed, and those who sought to rob him of the fruits of his labor took a bold stand. The result of all this was, that the inventor never received any just compensation for a machine that revolutionized the commerce of the country, and added enormously to the power and progress of the Republic. Lord Macaulay said that Eli Whitney did more to make the United States powerful than Peter the Great did to make the Russian Empire dominant. Robert Fulton declared that Arkwright, Watt, and Whitney were the three men that did more for mankind than any of their contemporaries. This is easy to believe, when we remember that while the South shipped 6 bags of cotton to England in 1786, and only 379 in 1791, ten years after the cotton gin came into use, 82,000 bales were exported. The very importance of Whitney's invention made it immensely profitable for the vicious and the depraved to seize and appropriate the inventor's rights. These robberies were upheld by those who were anxious to share in the profits; and political demagogues made themselves popular by misrepresenting Whitney, and clamoring against the law that was intended to protect him. It was only by means of this clamor, half political and wholly dishonest, that the plain rights of Whitney could be denied and justice postponed. His invention was entirely new. It was distinct from every other. It had no connection with and no relation to any other invention that had been made. It stood alone, and there could be no difficulty whatever in identifying it. And yet Whitney had just this difficulty. In his efforts to prove that he was the inventor of the cotton gin, and that he was entitled to a share of the immense profits that those who used it were reaping, he had to travel thousands of miles, and spend thousands of dollars in appearing before Legislatures and in courts that denied him justice. The life of his patent had nearly expired before any court finally enforced his right, and Congress refused to grant him an extension beyond the fourteen years that had then nearly expired.

Associations and combinations had been formed for the purpose of defrauding Whitney, and these were represented by the ablest lawyers that could be hired. It is no wonder that Whitney, in writing to Robert Fulton, a brother inventor, declared that the troubles he had to contend with were the result of a lack of desire on the part of mankind to see justice done. The truth is, his invention was of such prime importance that the public fought for its possession, and justice and honesty were for the moment lost sight of. At one time but a few men in Georgia were bold enough to go into court and testify to the simplest facts within their knowledge; and Whitney himself says, that in one instance he had the greatest difficulty in proving that the machine had been used in Georgia, although at that very moment three separate gins were at work within fifty yards of the building in which the court sat. They were all so near, that the rattle and hum of the machinery could be heard from the court-house steps.

In December, 1807, a judge was found to affirm the rights of Whitney under his patent. The judge's name was Johnson; and in his decision he said, " The whole interior of the Southern States was languishing, and its inhabitants emigrating for want of some object to engage their attention and employ their industry, when the invention of this machine at once opened views to them which set the whole country in active motion. From childhood to age it has presented to us a lucrative employment. Individuals who were depressed with poverty, and sunk in idleness, have suddenly risen to wealth and respectability. Our debts have been paid off. Our capital has increased, and our lands have trebled themselves in value. We cannot express the weight of the obligation which the country owes to this invention. The extent of it cannot now be seen."

The language of the learned judge was high-flown;
but he was a just judge, and he had a faint and glim-
mering idea of the real importance of this remarkable
invention. It was a very simple affair. The principle
came to Whitney in a flash, and he had a model con-
structed within ten days after the despairing planters
had gone to him with their problem. But it may be
doubted whether any other individual, by one simple
invention, ever did so much for the progress and en-
richment of human interests, and for the welfare and
the comfort of the human race. This little machine
made the agriculture of the South the strongest and
the richest in the world, and gave to this section a
political power that was for years supreme in the
nation, and was only surrendered as the result of a
long and exhausting war. By means of the cotton
gin, towns and cities have sprung up, and a vast net-
work of railways has been built; and yet the most that
Whitney received was a royalty on his gin in North
Carolina, and a donation of fifty thousand dollars from
the State of South Carolina. In Georgia his right to
his invention was stolen, and all that he got out of it
was a number of costly lawsuits.

After struggling for five years against the overwhelming odds that avarice and greed had mustered
to aid them, Whitney turned his attention in another
direction, and made a still more remarkable display of
his genius. This part of his career does not belong
directly to the history of Georgia, but it is interesting
enough to be briefly recorded here. The United States
Government was in want of arms, and this want various

contractors had failed to meet. Through the influence of the secretary of the treasury, Whitney was given a contract to make ten thousand muskets at $13.40 apiece. He had no capital, no works, no machinery, no tools, no skilled workmen, no raw material. In creating a part of these and commanding the rest, he called into play an inventive genius, the extent of which must always excite wonder and admiration.

Within ten years he created his own works, and invented and made his own tools, invented and made his own machinery. More than this, he invented and applied a wholly new principle of manufacture, — a principle that has done more to advance human industry and increase wealth all over the world than any other known effort of the human mind to solve material problems. He invented and developed the principle or system of making the various parts of a musket or any other complex manufactured article, such as the sewing machine, so absolutely uniform as to be interchangeable. This principle has been carried out in hundreds of thousands of different ways. It has entered into and become a feature of a vast range of manufactures. The principle was established by a series of inventions as wonderful as any that the human mind ever conceived, so that Whitney has been aptly called the Shakespeare of invention. His inventions remain practically unchanged. After ninety years of trial, they are found to be practically perfect.

It was his peculiar gift to be able to convey into inanimate machinery the skill that a human being could acquire only after years of study and practice.

It is almost like belittling the greatest of marvels to call it a stroke of genius. He made it possible for the most ordinary laborer to accomplish a hundred times as much in an hour, and with the most exquisite perfection, as a skilled laborer could accomplish in a day.

On these wonderful inventions Whitney took out no patents. He gave them all to the public. In this way he revenged himself on those who had successfully robbed him of the fruits of his labor and genius in the invention of the cotton gin. Perhaps if he had been more justly treated in Georgia, he might have set up his works in this State, and this fact might have made the South the seat of great manufacturing industries. Who knows?

SOME GEORGIA INVENTIONS.

THE credit of inventing the steamboat is by general consent given to Robert Fulton. Every school-boy is taught that such is the case, and yet the fact is at least very doubtful. There is preserved among the papers in the Archives of Georgia a document that indicates, that, while Robert Fulton has won the credit for an invention that has revolutionized the commerce of the world, the real inventor may have been William Longstreet of Augusta, an uncle of General James B. Longstreet, and the father of Judge A. B. Longstreet, author of "Georgia Scenes." On the 26th of September, 1790, William Longstreet sent the following letter to Edward Telfair, who was then governor of Georgia:—

SIR, — I make no doubt but you have heard of my steamboat and as often heard it laughed at. But in this I have only shared the fate of all other projectors, for it has uniformly been the custom of every country to ridicule even the greatest inventions until use has proved their utility.

My not reducing my scheme to practice has been a little unfortunate for me, I confess, and perhaps for the people in general, but until very lately I did not think that either artists or material could be had in the place sufficient. However, necessity, that grand science of invention, has furnished me with an idea of perfecting my plans almost entirely with wooden materials, and by such workmen as may be got here, and from a thorough confidence of its success, I have presumed to ask your assistance and patronage

Should it succeed agreeable to my expectations, I hope I shall discover that source of duty which such favors always merit, and should it not succeed, your reward must lay with other unlucky adventurers.

For me to mention to you all the advantages arising from such a machine would be tedious, and, indeed, quite unnecessary. Therefore I have taken the liberty to state in this plain and humble manner my wish and opinion, which I hope you will excuse, and I will remain, either with or without approbation,

Your Excellency's most obedient and very humble servant,

WILLIAM LONGSTREET.

There are two features of this letter that ought to attract attention. One is that William Longstreet has the name of "steamboat" as pat as if the machine were in common use. The second is his allusion to the fact that his conception of a boat to be propelled by steam was so well known as to be noised abroad.

Credit is sometimes given to John Fitch, who, it is said, invented a boat propelled by steam, that carried passengers on the Delaware River in 1787. An Englishman named Symington is said to have run a steamboat in 1801, while Robert Fulton's success was delayed until 1806. All these men have received credit for their efforts to benefit humanity, but history is silent in regard to William Longstreet. In one book about Georgia the remark is made that " James Longstreet is said to have invented the steamboat in 1793," but in this instance neither the name nor the date is correct.

In old St. Paul's churchyard in Augusta there is a tombstone which bears the inscription, " Sacred to the memory of William Longstreet, who departed this life September 1, 1814, aged 54 years, 10 months, and 26 days." Below this runs the pleasant legend, "All the days of the afflicted are evil, but he that is of a merry heart hath a continual feast." We are thus left to infer that William Longstreet was a man of a merry heart; and that fact is certified to by the cleverness with which his son, the author of "Georgia Scenes," has preserved for us some of the quaint characters that lived and moved and had their being on the borders of Georgia society directly after the Revolution.

Being an inventor, a man of ingenious ideas, and some-what ambitious of serv-ing the public in that way, William Long-street certainly had need of a merry heart; for, as he himself says, the way of the pro-jector is hard. The term itself is used in Georgia to this day to express a certain sort of good-natured contempt.

Go into the country places and ask after some acquaint-ance who has not prospered in a worldly way, and the answer will be, "Oh, he's just a prodjikin around."

It is certain that William Longstreet knew that steam could be used as a motive power long before it was so applied; and because he employed a good deal of his time in trying to discover the principle, he was ridiculed by his neighbors and friends, and the more thoughtless among them didn't know whether he was a crank, a half-wit, or a "luny." From all accounts, he was a modest, shy, retiring man, though a merry one. He had but little money to devote to the experiments he wished to make, and in this was not different from the great majority of inventors.

For a long time Longstreet's zeal and enthusiasm attracted the attention of a few of his wealthy friends, and these furnished him such money as he wanted; but no very long time was needed to convince those who were spending their money that the idea of propelling a boat by steam, instead of by sails or oars, was ridiculous. Longstreet made many experiments, but he had not hit upon the method of applying the principle he had in mind: consequently his rich friends closed their purses, and left him entirely to his own resources. A newspaper publication, in giving some of the facts in regard to Longstreet's efforts, says that he and his steamboat were made the subject of a comic song:—

> "Can you row the boat ashore,
>   Billy boy, Billy boy?
> Can you row the boat ashore,
>   Gentle Billy?
> Can you row the boat ashore
> Without a paddle or an oar,
>   Billy boy?"

Though he had failed many times, Longstreet was not disheartened. He continued his experiments, and at last succeeded in making a toy boat, which he exhibited to a few friends. His idea at this time, it seems, was not to construct a steamboat, but merely to convince some of his friends that steam could be used as a motive power. But in this he was not very successful. His toy boat did all that he wanted it to do; but his friends declared, that while steam might be used to move a small boat, it could never be used to move a large one. The experience of a new generation showed that there was one wise man in Augusta and a great many fools. Nevertheless William Longstreet determined to show that a large boat could be moved by a large amount of steam as easily as a small boat could be moved by a small volume.

Now, while he was making his experiments, and trying to overcome the difficulties that presented themselves, Robert Fulton was living in Paris with Joel Barlow. He was in Paris when Napoleon became first consul. At that time he was experimenting with his diving boat and submarine torpedo. Napoleon was so much interested in this work that he gave Fulton ten thousand francs to carry it on. The inventor was in France in 1803 when Napoleon organized his army for the invasion of England. He was surrounded by influential friends, and he had money at his command.

Compared with William Longstreet, Robert Fulton was "in clover." Longstreet was compelled to work without money, and in the midst of a community whose curiosity had developed into criticism and ridicule. Thus it was not until 1806 that he succeeded in completing a steamboat that would accommodate twenty or twenty-five persons. He went on board, accompanied by such of his friends as he could persuade, and in the presence of a curious and doubting crowd the first real steamboat was launched on the Savannah River. Some of the friends of those on board, feeling anxious for their safety if the "contraption" should explode, secured a skiff, and followed the steamboat at a safe distance, ready to pick up such of the passengers as might survive when the affair had blown to pieces. Longstreet headed the boat down the river, and went in that direction for several miles. Then he turned the head of the little boat upstream; and, although the current was swift, he carried his passengers back to the wharf, and several miles above.

From that hour William Longstreet became a man of some consequence in the community. Those who had ridiculed him now sang his praises, and those who had doubted that steam could be used as a motive power were now convinced. His friends tried hard to get him to go to Washington and secure the benefits of a patent for his invention; but he persistently refused to take any steps to profit by the results of his genius, or indeed to make his invention known. His constant reply to all those who tried to persuade him to go to Washington was, that he had carried on his experiments simply to prove the truth of his theory to his own satisfaction, and to convince those whose respect he coveted that he was neither a fool nor a crank.

Some of his friends and admirers were themselves preparing to go to Washington in behalf of the inventor, but they had put off their journey until the year after the exhibition was made in Augusta, and at that time they heard that Robert Fulton had exhibited his steamboat "Clermont" on the Hudson River. They then gave up their design, and William Longstreet continued to remain in the seclusion that was so pleasant to him.

It is a noteworthy fact, that twelve years after William Longstreet made his successful experiments on the Savannah River, Georgia enterprise built, launched, and managed the first steamship that ever crossed the ocean. This great enterprise was organized in Savannah in 1818. The Georgia Company contracted to have the ship built in New York; and when completed, it was named the "Savannah." The vessel was finished and brought to Savannah in April, 1819. In May the steamship left Savannah bound for Liverpool. From Liverpool it went to St. Petersburg, and then returned to Savannah, having made the voyage in fifty days.

The first sewing machine was invented by Rev. Frank R. Goulding, a Georgian who has won fame among the children of the land as the author of "The Young Marooners." He invented the sewing machine for the purpose of lightening the labors of his wife; and she used it for some years before some other genius invented it, or some traveler stole the idea and improved on it.

Dr. Crawford W. Long, in 1842, when twenty-seven years of age, performed the first painless surgical operation that is known to history. In 1839, Velpeau of Paris declared that the attempts to find some agent by which to prevent pain in surgical operations was nothing less than chimerical; and as late as 1846 Sir Benjamin Brodie said, "Physicians and surgeons have been looking in vain, from the days of Hippocrates down to the present time, for the means of allaying or preventing bodily pain." And yet three years after the declaration of Velpeau, and four years before the statement of Sir Benjamin Brodie, the young Georgia physician had removed a tumor from the neck of a patient, and that patient had felt no pain.

The story is very interesting. Dr. Crawford W. Long was born in Danielsville, Madison County, Ga., on the 1st of November, 1815. He graduated at

the University of Georgia, studied medicine, and graduated at the medical department of the University of Pennsylvania. He then went to Jefferson, Jackson County, where he opened an office, and practiced medicine for many years.

In those days the young men living in the country districts, for want of something better to amuse them, were in the habit of inhaling nitrous-oxide gas, or, as it was then popularly known, "laughing gas." The young people would gather together, and some of them would inhale the gas until they came under its influence. The result was in most cases very amusing. Some would laugh, some would cry, and all in various ways would carry out the peculiarities of their characters and dispositions. Thus, if a young man had an inward inclination to preach, he would, under the influence of "laughing gas," proceed to deliver a sermon. As these "laughing-gas" parties were exhilarating to the young people who inhaled the gas, and amusing to those who were spectators, they became very popular.

But it was not always easy to secure the gas. On one occasion a company of young men went to Dr. Long's office and asked him to make them a supply of "laughing gas." There was no apparatus in the office suitable for making it, but Dr. Long told the young men that the inhalation of sulphuric ether would have the same effect. He had become acquainted with this property of ether while studying medicine in Philadelphia. The young men and their friends were so well pleased with the effects of ether inhalation, that "ether parties" became fashionable in that section, as well as in other parts of the State. At these ether parties, Dr. Long noticed that persons who received injuries while under its influence felt no pain. On one occasion a young man received an injury to his ankle joint that disabled him for several days, and he told Dr. Long that he did not feel the slightest pain until the effects of the ether had passed off. Observing these facts, Dr. Long was led to believe that surgical operations might be performed without pain.

Dr. Long's theory was formed in 1841, but he waited for some time before testing it, in the hope that a case of surgery of some importance — the amputation of an arm or a leg — might fall in his practice. On the 30th of March, 1842, Dr. Long removed a tumor from the neck of Mr. James M. Venable. On the 6th of June, the same year, another small tumor was removed from the neck of the same patient, and both operations were painless. Mr. Venable inhaled sulphuric ether, and the effect of it was to render him insensible to the pain of cutting out the tumors.

Dr. Long had told Mr. Venable that he would charge little or nothing for removing the tumors under the influence of ether. The bill rendered for both operations amounted to $4.50; but, small as the bill was, it represented the discovery and application of ether in surgical practice, — one of the greatest boons to mankind. Up to that time no patient under the surgeon's knife had ever been able to escape the horror and pain of an operation.

Dr. Long did not at once print the facts about his discovery. He wanted to make assurance doubly sure. He waited in the hope of having an important case of surgery under his charge, such as the amputation of a leg or an arm. But these cases, rare at any time, were still rarer at that time, especially in the region where Dr. Long practiced. He finally satisfied himself, however, of the importance of his discovery, but, having waited until 1846, found that at least three persons — Wells, Jackson, and Morton — had hit on the same discovery, and had made publication of it. Morton patented ether under the name of "Letheon," and in October, 1846, administered it to a patient in the Massachusetts General Hospital.

In 1844, Horace Wells, a native of Vermont, discovered that the inhalation of nitrous-oxide gas produces anæsthesia. He was a dentist. He gave it to his patients, and was able to perform dental operations without causing pain. Thus we may see how the case stands. Long produced anæsthesia in 1842; that is to say, he caused his patients to inhale sulphuric ether in that year, whenever he had a painful operation to perform, and in each case the operation was painless.

In 1846, when the surgeons of the Massachusetts General Hospital performed painless operations on patients, after administering to them Morton's patented "Letheon," which was his name for sulphuric ether, there came about a great war of pamphlets, and it ended tragically. Long had never made any secret of the substance which he used. He gave information of it to all the surgeons and doctors with whom he came in contact; and he was not in any way concerned in the conflict that was carried on by Jackson, Morton, and Wells. He simply gathered together the facts of his discovery, proved that he was the first physician to perform painless operations in surgery, and that was the end of it so far as he was concerned.

Wells became insane, and committed suicide in New York in 1848. Morton died in New York City of congestion of the brain. Jackson ended his days in an insane asylum.

In Boston a monument has been erected to the discoverer of anæsthesia. The name of Crawford W. Long should stand first upon it, and should be followed by the names of Wells, Morton, and Jackson.

THE EARLY PROGRESS OF THE STATE.

AFTER the invention of the cotton gin, the progress of the people and the development of the agriculture of the State went forward very rapidly. The population began to increase. The movement of families from Virginia and North Carolina grew constantly larger. In Virginia, and in settled portions of North Carolina, it was found that the soil and climate were not favorable to the growth of the cotton plant: consequently hundreds of families left their homes in these States, and came to Georgia.

When Oglethorpe settled the Colony, the charter under which he acted prohibited the introduction and use of negro slaves in the Colony. It is hard to say at

this late day whether this portion of the charter was
dictated by feelings of humanity, especially when we remember that in those days, and in most of the Colonies,
there were many white people — men, women, and children — employed and used as slaves. From the very
first, many of the Georgia colonists were anxious to
introduce negro slaves, but the trustees firmly refused
to allow it. There was a strong party in favor of introducing negroes, and those who opposed the movement
presently found themselves in a very small and unpopular minority. By 1748 the excitement over the question
had grown so great, that those colonists who were opposed to negro slavery were compelled to abandon their
position. Rev. Mr. Whitefield, the eloquent preacher,
had already bought and placed negro slaves at his
Orphan House at Bethesda, near Savannah. The colonists had also treated this part of the charter with
contempt. They pretended to hire negroes' homes in
South Carolina for a hundred years, or during life.
They paid the "hire" in advance, the sum being the
full value of the slaves. Finally negroes were bought
openly from traders in Savannah. Some of them were
seized; but a majority of the magistrates were in favor
of the introduction of negroes, and they were able to
postpone legal decisions from time to time.

Rev. George Whitefield, whose wonderful eloquence
has made his name famous, and Hon. James Habersham, had great influence with the trustees; and it was
mainly due to their efforts that the colonists were
legally allowed to purchase and use negro slaves. Mr.
Habersham affirmed that the Colony could not prosper

without slave labor.   Rev. Mr. Whitefield, on the other hand, was in favor of negro slavery on the broad ground of philanthropy.   He boldly declared that it would be of great advantage to the African to be brought from his barbarous surroundings and placed among civilized Christians.   When we remember what has happened, who can deny that the remark of the eloquent preacher was not more to the purpose, and nearer to the truth, than some of the modern statements about American slavery?   What really happened (as any one may discover by looking into impartial history) was, that thousands of negroes who had been captured in battle, and made slaves of in their own country, were taken from that dark land and brought into the light of Christian civilization.   Their condition, mentally and morally, was so improved, that, in little more than a century after Whitefield made his statement, the government of the United States ventured to make citizens of them.   The contrast between their condition and that of the negroes who remained in Africa is so startling, that a well-known abolitionist, writing twenty years after emancipation, has described slavery as a great university, which the negroes entered as barbarians, and came out of as Christians and citizens.

The efforts of the Colony to secure a repeal of the act prohibiting slavery were successful.   The trustees in London concluded that it would be better to permit slavery, with such restrictions and limitations as might be proper, than to permit the wholesale violations that were then going on; and so in 1749 the colonists of Georgia were allowed by law to own and use negro slaves.

Thus, when the cotton gin came fairly into use, slavery had been legally allowed in Georgia for nearly half a century. The rest of the Colonies had long enjoyed that privilege. The cotton gin, therefore, had a twofold effect, — it increased the cotton crop and the value of the lands, and it also increased the use of negro slaves. The Virginians and North Carolinians, who came to Georgia, brought their slaves with them; and the Georgians, as their crops became profitable, laid out their surplus cash in buying more negroes. The slave trade became very prosperous, and both Old England and New England devoted a large amount of capital and enterprise to this branch of commerce.

As the population increased, and the cotton crop became more valuable, the demand for land became keener. To this fact was due the intense excitement kindled by the Yazoo Fraud in 1794. The cotton gin had been introduced the year before, and the people were beginning to see and appreciate the influence the invention would have on their prosperity. Instead of selling land to speculators, they wanted to keep it for themselves and children, or at least to get something like its real value.

The cotton gin had increased not only the demand for negro slaves, but also the demand for land; and indirectly it was the cause of the various troubles the State had with the Indians after the close of the War for Independence. The troubles with the Indians also led finally to serious misunderstandings between the United States Government and that of Georgia. In May, 1796, a treaty was made between the United

States and the Creeks. This treaty created some indignation among the people, and was denounced as an
interference by the General Government with State
affairs. The lands which the Indians ceded to the
United States were a part of the Territory of Georgia,
and the transaction gave rise to much discussion and
considerable bad feeling.

In ten years, from 1790 to 1800, the population in
Georgia had increased more than eighty thousand.
During the next ten years the increase in the population was more than ninety thousand. This increase
meant a still greater demand for farm lands. Westward the Territory of Georgia extended to the Mississippi River. The agitation which began over this
rich possession when the Yazoo Fraud was attempted,
was kept up until 1800, when Georgia appointed four
of her most prominent citizens to meet with commissioners appointed by the United States, and settle all
questions that had arisen. The result was, that Georgia
ceded to the General Government all her lands belonging to the State, south of Tennessee and west of the
Chattahoochee River. These lands were to be sold,
and out of the proceeds the State was to receive $1,250,-
000. It was also provided that the United States, at
its own expense, should extinguish the Indian titles
to the lands held by the Creeks between the forks of
the Oconee and Ocmulgee rivers, and that in like manner the General Government should extinguish the
Indian title to all the other lands within the State of
Georgia. Under this agreement, and the Indian treaty
based upon it, nearly all of the lands lying between the

Oconee and Ocmulgee rivers were opened up for occupation and cultivation.

All the Territory of Georgia was looked upon by the people as a public domain, belonging to the State for distribution among the citizens. The lands east of the Oconee were divided among the people under the plan known as the "Head Right System." By this system every citizen was allowed to choose, and survey to suit himself, a body of unoccupied land. This done, he received a title called a "head right land warrant," which was issued to him when he paid a small fee and a nominal price for the land. If no one had previously appropriated the same land, the warrant was his title. But much confusion arose in the distribution of titles, and serious disputes grew out of it. The poorer sections of land were neglected, and only the most fertile sections surveyed.

When the lands west of the Oconee were acquired, the clumsy Head Right System was given up for what is known as the "Land Lottery System." "All free white males, twenty-one years of age or older, every married man with children under age, widows with children, and all families of orphan minors," were allowed to draw in the lottery. Lists of these persons were made out in each county, and sent to the governor. The lottery was drawn under the management of five responsible persons. The tickets to be drawn were marked with the numbers of the land lots, and these were put into boxes with numerous blanks. Those who were fortunate enough to draw numbered tickets were entitled to plats and grants of their lots, signed by the governor.

The lots were not all of the same size. Some contained 202½ acres, others 490 acres. Twelve months after the drawing was completed, the fortunate person was required to pay into the State treasury four dollars for every hundred acres contained in his lot.

Many of those who had the good fortune to draw prizes in the land-lottery scheme paid the necessary amount of money, and received titles to their land lots; but many others neglected to pay in the money, and thus forfeited their titles.

It has been said that the land hunger of the people at this time was both selfish and sordid; but if we come to look at the matter closely, selfishness is behind much of the material progress that the world has made. The selfishness of individuals is not more conspicuous than the selfishness of communities, commonwealths, and nations. In history we find the rumseller, the land grabber, and the speculator following hard upon the heels of the missionary. The selfishness of nations is frequently given the name of " patriotism," and rightly so, since it is a movement for the good of all.

When Georgia had fairly begun to recover from the disastrous results of the War for Independence, the troubles that resulted in the War of 1812 began to make themselves felt. France and England were at war; and the United States Government tried to remain neutral, giving aid to neither the one nor the other. But this was not pleasing to either of these great powers. Both were interested in the trade and commerce of this country, and both issued orders affecting American affairs. The United States resented the interference, and protested against it. Great Britain, with an arrogance made bitter by the remembrance of her humiliating defeat at the hands of a few feeble Colonies, replied to the American protest, declaring that American ships would still be searched, and American sailors impressed into the service of the British, wherever found on the high seas. In 1807 a British man-of-war fired on an American merchant vessel as it was leaving harbor. Three men were killed, eighteen wounded, and four sailors seized. This outrage inflamed the whole country, and in December of that year Congress passed a law preventing American vessels from  leaving their ports to trade with foreign nations. This law was deeply resented by the New England States, and they held at Hartford, Conn., the first secession convention that ever met in this country.

Georgia was foremost among the States to denounce and resist the aggressive acts of Great Britain. In 1808 the Legislature sent an address to the President of the United States, approving the measures he had taken, and declared that the people of Georgia were strong in their independence, and proud of their government, and that they would never wish to see the lives and property of their brethren exposed to the insult and rapacity of a foreign power; but if the war should come, they would, in proportion to their number. and resources, give zealous aid to the government of their choice.

The British, meanwhile, made arrangements to force a cotton trade with Georgia and South Carolina, and for the purpose fitted out a number of vessels of from ten to fifteen guns each. These vessels were to be employed in opening the ports of Georgia and Carolina. A war brig anchored at Tybee, and two of its officers went to Savannah. When they had made known their purpose, they were peremptorily ordered away. They returned to their vessel and put to sea; but as they were leaving, they fired at a pilot boat in the harbor, and committed other outrages.

This incident and others aroused the indignation of the people. The Legislature passed resolutions, addressed to the President of the United States, declaring that all hope of a peaceful termination of the difficulty had been lost, that the duty of the United States was to maintain its sovereign rights against the despots of Europe, and that the citizens of Georgia would ever be found in readiness to assert the rights and support the dignity of the country whenever called on by the General Government. By the time the treaty of peace was made, the day before Christmas in 1814, the war spirit in Georgia had been roused to the highest pitch by the numerous outrages committed by the Indian allies of the British.

But the story of the Indian troubles belongs to a chapter by itself.

I F all the stories of the troubles of the early settlers of Georgia with the Indians could be written out, they would fill a very large book.   All the whites with whom the red men came in contact in Georgia were not as just, as generous, and as unselfish as James Edward Oglethorpe.   On the other hand, not all the Indians with whom the whites had dealings were as wise and as honest as old Tomochichi.   Consequently misunderstandings arose, and prejudices grew and developed. This was greatly helped by dishonest traders and speculators, who were keen to take advantage of the ignorance of the Indians.

The controlling influence among the Indians in Georgia was the Creek Confederacy (or nation); and

this, in turn, was practically controlled by the Musco-
gees. North of the Creeks, Broad River being the
dividing line, lived the Cherokees, a nation even more
warlike than the Creeks. The impression made upon
the Indians by Oglethorpe and some of his more prudent successors, made them the strong friends of the
British. Of course, the red men were unable to appreciate the merits of the quarrel between the Georgia
settlers and King George: but, even if matters had
been different, they would probably have remained on
friendly terms with the Royalists; for Governor Wright,
who was a wise as well as a good man, took great
pains, when the Liberty Boys began their agitations
against the Crown, to conciliate the Indians, and to
show them that the King was their friend. What was
known as "the royal presents" were promptly sent
from England, and promptly delivered to and distributed among the Indians. The governor sent for the
chiefs, and had conferences with them; so that when
the Revolution began, the Upper and the Lower Creeks,
and the Cherokees as well, were the firm friends of the
British. During the Revolution, as we have already
seen, they made constant and unprovoked attacks on
the patriots, burning their houses, carrying off their
cattle, and murdering their helpless women and children. These raids were continued even after the Americans had compelled Great Britain to recognize their
independence, and hundreds of incidents might be given
to show the ferocity with which the savages attacked
the whites. In many cases the settlements were compelled to build stockades, in which the people took

shelter, for safety as well as defense, whenever there was an alarm.

On one occasion shortly after the close of the war, the Indians attacked the family of a man named William Tyner, who was living in what is known as Elbert County. Tyner himself was absent, and his family was entirely without protection. Mrs. Tyner was killed, the brains of her youngest child were dashed out against a tree, and another child was scalped and left for dead. A young boy named Noah, the son of Mr. Tyner, escaped in the general confusion, and hid himself in a hollow tree. This tree was for many years known as "Noah's Ark." Mary and Tamar, two daughters, were suffered to live; but the Indians carried them off to the Coweta towns on the Chattahoochee. These children remained with the Indians several years. John Manack, an Indian trader, saw them there, and purchased Mary. He then brought her to Elbert County, and afterwards made her his wife. He returned to the Indian nation shortly afterwards, and tried to purchase Tamar; but, as she was useful to the Indians in bringing wood and fuel for their fires, they refused to sell her. When Manack went away, an old Indian woman, who was fond of Tamar, learned that the Indians, suspecting the girl was preparing to escape, had decided to burn her at the stake. The old woman helped her to escape by providing her with provisions and a canoe. She also gave Tamar directions how to go down the Chattahoochee. By day the fleeing girl hid herself in the thick swamps along the banks of the river, and by night she floated down the river in her canoe. She finally reached Apalachicola Bay, took passage on a vessel, and shortly afterwards arrived at Savannah. Here she was assisted to her home in Elbert County by the citizens. She married a man named Hunt, and no doubt many of her descendants are still living in Georgia.

There was once an Indian village in Troup County, on the west bank of the Chattahoochee, where the Indians who lived on the Alabama side of the river were in the habit of meeting before and after their raids upon the white settlements. Before the raids they would meet there to arrange their programme; and afterwards they would assemble at the village to count the scalps they had taken, dispose of their prisoners, and divide the spoils. On one occasion, after a very destructive raid into the white settlements, the Indians returned to this village, and began to celebrate the success with which they had been able to creep upon the settlements at dead of night, murder the unsuspecting whites, burn their dwellings, and drive off their horses and cattle. This time, however, the Indians had been followed by a few hundred men, under the leadership of General David Adams, who was at that time a major in the militia, and a scout. Major Adams had taken part in the closing scenes of the Revolution when quite a young man. When the Creeks renewed their depredations after the war, Major Adams, both as a scout and as a leader, fought the Indians with such success as to win distinction.

He followed the Indians on this occasion with a few

hundred men, who had volunteered to accompany him. His pursuit was not active. The men under him were not seasoned soldiers; and even if they had been, the force of Indians was too large to justify an attack. Major Adams followed the Indians in the hope that he and his men would find an opportunity to surprise them. The Indians marched straight for the village on the west bank of the Chattahoochee, about eight miles beyond the point where La Grange now stands. At this village, which was the central point of the Lower Creek nation at that time, there were many Indians — men, women, and children — awaiting the return of the raiders. It was in the late afternoon when they reached the village, and as the sun went down they began the celebration of their victories; and in this they were joined by the Indians, who had been waiting for their return.

Major Adams had halted his command a few miles from the river, where he waited until night fell. He then advanced silently to the banks of the stream, which was not so wide that he and his men could not see the Indians dancing around their fires, and hear their whoops and yells. On one bank stood the men whose families and friends had been murdered; on the opposite shore, and almost within a stone's throw, the red murderers danced and howled in savage delight.

For half the night, at least, the orgies were kept up by the Indians; but at last they grew weary of the song and dance. Their fires slowly died out, and there came a moment when the whites, who were watching and waiting, could hear nothing but the murmur of the flowing water, as it rippled over the shoals or lapped the bank. The time had come to strike a blow, if a blow was to be struck. It was characteristic of Major Adams, that, instead of sending one of his little party to find out the position of the village and its surroundings, so as to be able to make a swift, sudden, and an effective attack, he himself proposed to go.

It was a hazardous undertaking, and required a bold heart to undertake it. Major Adams knew there was a ford near the point where his men lay. The trail led into the river; but, once in the river, it was lost. He had to find the ford for himself, and it proved to be a very narrow and difficult one. It led in a direct line across the river nearly halfway, and then turned down the stream in an oblique direction. A part of the ford was over a slippery shoal. At some points the water was knee-deep, at others it was chin-deep.

With great difficulty Major Adams reached the opposite bank in safety. The paths leading from the ford into the swamp that lay between the Indian village and the river were so numerous that the stout-hearted scout hardly knew which one to take. He chose one almost at random, and, after following it through the thick underbrush, he found that it had led him some distance below the village. He followed the margin of the swamp back again, and soon found himself in the outskirts of the village. There he paused to listen. A dog somewhere in the settlement barked uneasily and sleepily.

Pushing forward, but moving with the utmost caution, Major Adams soon found himself in the center of the village. In every hut the Indians were sleeping; and, in addition to these, the ground seemed to be covered with warriors, who lay stretched out and snoring, their rifles and tomahawks within easy reach. The brave Georgian went through the village from one end to the other. Once a huge Indian, near whom he was passing, raised himself on his elbow, grasped his gun, and looked carefully in every direction. Having satis-

fied himself, he lay down, and was soon snoring again. Fortunately, Major Adams had seen the Indian stir, and sank to the ground near a group of sleeping warriors, where he remained until he was sure the savage was asleep.

He had examined every point of attack and defense in the village, and was returning to the river, when he saw a pony tethered to a sapling. Thinking that the little animal would be able to find the ford without trouble, and could thus be used as a safe guide, Major Adams resolved to capture it. He approached the pony with that intention, but not until too late did he discover that it had a bell hung on its neck. The pony, frightened at the sight of a white man, broke the rope by which he was tied, and went scampering through the village, arousing and alarming warriors, squaws, children, and dogs with the jingling bell.

At the sound of the bell, Major Adams knew that there would be a tremendous uproar in the village, and he made an instant rush toward the river, but soon found himself entangled in the briers and thick underbrush of the swamp. It was fortunate that he missed the path leading to the ford; for a party of Indians ran in that direction, either to catch the pony, or to find out whether they were about to be attacked. Some of them passed within a few feet of the spot where Major Adams stood.

In a short time the Indians returned to the village, and it was not long before everything was as quiet and as peaceful as before the uproar. Major Adams, instead of hunting for the path, made his way directly to the river, slipped into the water, and swam straight across to the opposite bank. He soon found his men, and told them of his adventure and of the plans he had matured. Up to this moment he had been second in command. A colonel of militia was with the party, and it was his right to be the leader of the expedition; but now the men declared that they would cross the river under the leadership of no one but Adams. It was Adams or nobody; and the militia colonel, as gracefully as he could, yielded to the demand.

Major Adams led the volunteers safely across the treacherous ford and into the Indian town. The surprise was complete. Scarcely a warrior escaped. The women and children were spared as far as possible, but the village was burned to the ground. In retreat-ing from that point, which was the center of the famous Muscogee nation, Major Adams made long marches during the day, and camped without fires at night, and in this way brought his command out of the Indian country without the loss of a man.

But Adams's excursion to the center of the Muscogee (or Creek) nation did not settle matters. The troubles continued. The temper of the people was not improved by the efforts of the United States Government to take affairs into its own hands. In some instances the agents of the General Government sought to stir up active strife between the people of the State and the Indians, and it was their habit to belittle the State government by speaking of it contemptuously before the Indians. In many instances the United States stepped in between the agents of the State and the Indians, and prevented settlements and treaties that would have been of lasting benefit to both the whites and the Indians. This was not due to any purpose or desire of the General Government to trample on the rights of the State, but grew altogether out of the folly of the agents, who wanted to put on airs and advertise their importance.

In 1796 there was a treaty of peace arranged be-tween the Creek nation and the United States. Three commissioners represented the General Government, and Georgia also had three present; but the business was conducted without regard to the wishes of the Georgia commissioners, and, as the commissioners thought, without regard to the interests of the State. Seagrove was the name of the agent representing the General Government at that time, and his attitude toward Georgia was not calculated to give the Indians any respect for the commonwealth. After the treaty was signed, General James Jackson, on the part of Georgia, made an eloquent speech, in which he showed that the Creeks had not faithfully observed the treaties they had made with the State. He exhibited two schedules of property which they had stolen, amounting in value to $110,000, and demanded its restoration. When General Jackson had concluded, one of the prominent chiefs of the Creeks remarked that he could fill more paper than Jackson showed with a list of outrages of the Georgians upon his people. There was something more than a grain of truth in this; but on that very account the Indians and the Georgians should have been allowed to settle their difficulties in their own way, without the interference of the United States.

The result of the treaty at Coleraine, in 1796, was, that the Georgia agents were offended with Seagrove (the Indian agent for the United States), offended with the Indians, and displeased with the United States commissioners. To these last the Georgians presented a protest in which the Federal commissioners were accused of disregarding the interests of Georgia. Charges were brought against Seagrove, who, it was claimed, had influenced the Creeks not to cede the lands as far as the Ocmulgee. A bitter controversy grew out of this. It was, in fact, very nearly the beginning of the discussion that has continued from that day to this, in some shape or other, over the rights of the States and the power of the General Government. Pickett, in his "History of Alabama and Georgia," says that General Jackson, and Seagrove the Indian agent, became enemies, and afterwards fought a duel.

Other treaties were made with the Creeks up to 1806, but all these were violated when the Indians became the allies of the British during the War of 1812. It is only fair to the Indians to say that the leader in whom they placed the greatest confidence was a man who for many years nourished hot resentment against the United States, and especially against Georgia. This man was General Alexander McGillivray, who became famous as an opponent of the Americans and the Georgians in all their efforts to come to a just, fair, and peaceable understanding with the Creeks.

As has been stated, when the War of 1812 began, the Creeks became the allies of the British, and the attacks they made on the unprotected settlements were so numerous and so serious as to call for some action on the part of the General Government. In September, 1813, Congress called for a levy of Georgia troops, and the State authorities ordered 3,600 men to assemble at Camp Hope, near Fort Hawkins, on the Ocmulgee River. The ruins of Fort Hawkins may be seen to this day on the Ocmulgee, in the city of Macon.

The men who assembled at Camp Hope were volunteers, and all eager for service. The command of this force fell to General John Floyd, who made haste to take charge, and endeavored to make arrangements for taking the field at once. He found his men assembled according to orders, and all anxious to be led against the hostile Indians. But the little army could not march. The Federal Government had failed to supply the necessary funds. What is called "red tape" stood in the way of prompt action. A dispute arose. Federal officials placed the blame on the contractors who were to furnish supplies, and the contractors placed it on the officials, who had failed to furnish the necessary money. While this dispute was raging, General Floyd, who was a brave and gallant spirit, applied to the State Legislature, then in session, for a loan of $20,000. The request was granted, and he was able to equip his troops, procure supplies, and march into the country of the Creeks, by the middle or latter part of November.

Meanwhile the hostile Creeks had already challenged Georgia and begun their attack. On the 30th of August, seven hundred and twenty-five Creek Indians attacked Fort Mims on the Chattahoochee. The attack was as sudden as it was unexpected. It was made at twelve o'clock in the day, and the inmates of the fort were taken entirely by surprise. The savages massacred nearly three hundred men, women, and children in the most cruel manner. This horrible outrage spread consternation on the frontier, and aroused indignation in all parts of the country. Hundreds of frontier settlers fled from their homes, and sought safety in the more thickly settled regions.

It was owing to this massacre that the troops commanded by General Floyd were called out. This active and energetic leader began his campaign by building a line of forts and blockhouses from the Ocmulgee to the Alabama River, and in this way completely protected the northern part of the State from invasion by the Creeks. General Floyd accomplished this work in spite of the failure of the United States officials to supply with provisions and transportation the troops they had called out.

He completed his line of defense by building Fort Mitchell. Leaving a sufficient garrison in this fort, General Floyd placed himself at the head of nine hundred and fifty men, and marched on Autossee, one of the most populous towns of the Creek nation, situated on the left bank of the Tallapoosa River, and near the town of Tallassee, which was nearly as large. The distance from Fort Mitchell to Autossee was sixty miles, and General Floyd made it by forced night marches, resting his troops during the day. He was accompanied on this expedition by General William McIntosh, the famous Indian chief, who led four hundred friendly Creeks.

Arriving at Autossee and Tallassee at daybreak on the 29th of November, 1813, General Floyd arranged and ordered a simultaneous attack on both towns. By nine o'clock the Indians had been defeated and driven from the towns, and their houses burned. Four hundred houses were burned, with all the provisions and stock. Two hundred Indians were killed, including the kings of both towns. The pipe which the old chief of Tallassee had smoked at a treaty forty years before, was taken and presented to the governor, who placed it in the executive office of the State Capitol. Eleven whites were killed, and fifty-four wounded; among them, General Floyd himself, who had received a ball in the knee early in the fight. He refused to have his wound dressed, and continued on horseback, directing his troops, until after the battle was over. He never entirely recovered from the effects of this wound. After the towns had been entirely destroyed, the troops returned to Fort Mitchell, having marched a hundred and twenty miles in bitter cold weather, and fought a severe engagement on five days' provisions.

In January, 1814, General Floyd heard that the Upper Creeks had collected in great force at the Indian town of Hothlewaulee. By that time his wound had so far healed that he was able to ride a horse, and he determined to make an attack on the town. For this purpose he detached from the troops at Fort Mitchell a force of fifteen hundred men. The weather was cold, and the winter rains had so obstructed the roads that the troops found the march a weary and a difficult one; but they pressed on, nevertheless, cheered by the energy and enthusiasm of their gallant leader. They marched to within fifteen or twenty miles of the town, and there encamped. Between midnight and day a large body of Indians, led by the warrior Weatherford and Colonel Woodbine, an English officer, attacked General Floyd's camp. His troops were taken by surprise, but they were not demoralized. They had been fighting for six months, and were seasoned to all the dangers of Indian warfare. Above all, they had a leader who possessed in a wonderful degree a genius for war.

No sooner had the alarm been sounded than General Floyd rallied his little army, formed it in a square, the baggage in the center, and held the savages at bay until daylight. There was no faltering in any part of the line or on any side of the square. The dauntless courage of Floyd himself seemed to control every man, down to the humblest private. When day dawned, a charge was sounded, and Floyd's troops drove the Indians before them at the point of the bayonet. Within a quarter of an hour after the charge was made, the battle was won. The loss of the Indians was never discovered, as they had an opportunity to carry off their killed and wounded up to the moment the charge was sounded. Seventeen Georgians were killed, and a hundred and thirty-two wounded. Floyd's camp was known as Camp Defiance, but in the official report the fight is called the battle of Chalibbee. The attack was made on Floyd in order to prevent a junction between his troops and those of General Andrew Jackson, who was fighting the Indians in the lower part of Alabama. The result of the fight made a junction unnecessary; and shortly afterwards the term for which Floyd's Georgia troops had enlisted expired, and they were discharged.

In 1814, when peace was declared between the United States and Great Britain, the Creeks remained quiet for some time.

TWO FAMOUS INDIAN CHIEFS.

A MONG the Indian leaders who made Georgia the scene of their operations, the most celebrated were General Alexander McGillivray and General William McIntosh. If these men had been born and brought up among the whites, both of them would have won lasting renown. They possessed the energy and the genius: all they lacked was the opportunity to direct their gifts into channels that would have benefited humanity.

Alexander McGillivray was one of the most remarkable men of his time, whether we regard him as a leader of the Indians or simply as an individual. His father, Lachlan McGillivray, being a lad of adventurous turn, ran away from a home in Scotland where he enjoyed all the advantages and comforts that wealth could give him, took passage on a ship bound for South Carolina, and shortly afterwards landed at Charleston. Wandering about in that city, and enjoying the sights that were new to his experience, he soon found himself in the suburbs of the city. There he found the headquarters of the Indian traders, who came to Charleston with their pack horses to carry merchandise of all kinds to the red men. One of these traders persuaded young McGillivray to go with him. His Scotch eye and mind were quick to appreciate the possibilities of this new business, and in a few years he became one of the most enterprising and prosperous of the Indian traders. He pushed his trade farther than any of his predecessors had ever dared to go. He went, indeed, to the neighborhood of Fort Toulouse. A few miles above that fort, where Wetumpka, Ala., now stands, he met Sehoy Marchand, a beautiful girl of about sixteen years. This girl was the daughter of Captain Marchand, who had commanded at Fort Toulouse, but who had been killed by his own soldiers in August, 1722. The soldiers rose against the officers of the garrison on account of the failure of France to forward money and supplies to the troops in her American settlement. The girl's mother was a Creek woman of the tribe of The Wind, the most powerful and influential family in the Creek nation. The young Scotchman fell in love with the dark-haired maiden, and she fell in love with the blue-eyed Scotchman, with his fair skin and red hair. Lachlan McGillivray built him a trading house on the Coosa, not far away, and soon married Sehoy, and carried her home. He became very wealthy. He owned two plantations on the Savannah River, which were well stocked with negroes, and stores filled with merchandise in both Savannah and Augusta. When Lachlan McGillivray's son Alexander reached the age of fourteen, he was carried to Savannah and placed at school, and in a few years was made a clerk in a counting-house at Savannah.

But the humdrum business of buying, selling, and adding up long rows of tiresome figures, did not please him, and so he neglected his duties to read books, mainly histories. His father, taking the advice of friends, placed young Alexander under the tutorship of a clergyman in Charleston, where the lad learned Latin and Greek, and in that way became well grounded in what our dear old grandfathers called polite literature. But one day word came to the young man that the chiefs of the Creek nation, who were getting into trouble with the people of Georgia, were waiting for the moment when he, as a descendant of the tribe of The Wind, should return and take charge of the affairs of the nation. So he departed suddenly from Charleston, and turned his horse's head toward the wilderness.

On his way to the Creek nation, he fell in with Leclerc Milfort, an adventurous Frenchman, who afterwards wrote a book of travels, and was made a general of brigade by Napoleon. Milfort married one of McGillivray's sisters, was made Tustenuggee (or grand war chief), and was the right-hand man of his powerful brother-in-law. The first that was heard of McGillivray after he left Charleston, he was presiding at a grand national council of the Creeks at the town of Coweta on the Chattahoochee. When Alexander arrived among the Creeks, Colonel Tait of the British army was stationed on the Coosa, and he used all his tact and influence to prevail upon the young man to take the side of the English in the war that was then going on between the Colonies and the mother country. To this end Colonel Tait pursued McGillivray with attentions, loaded him with favors, and finally caused him to be given the rank and pay of a colonel in the army. The result was that the great chief was throughout the war devoted to the cause of the British. This would have been natural in any event, for his father was a stanch Royalist. During the war, McGillivray frequently acted in concert with the notorious Daniel McGirth, sometimes leading his Indians in person; but his main dependence was on his brother-in-law Milfort, who was possessed of the most daring spirit. McGillivray preferred to plan and engage in intrigue, which gave the remarkable powers of his mind full play.

There is no doubt that the authorities of Georgia made a great mistake, after the war, in neglecting to win the friendship of McGillivray. Such a course would have prevented much suffering and bloodshed. The father of the great chief, Lachlan McGillivray, was living in Savannah at the close of the Revolution; and when the British were compelled to evacuate the city, he scraped together an immense amount of money and other valuables, and sailed for Scotland. He abandoned his plantations and negroes, in the hope that his wife and three children might be permitted to inherit them; but the Georgians confiscated the whole of the valuable estate, and thus the Creek leader had another reason for entertaining a bitter prejudice against the Whigs.

The result was, that until the day of his death, which occurred in 1792, he succeeded in baffling all the efforts of the Federal and State authorities to come to an understanding with the Creek nation. He was perhaps the most accomplished diplomat in the country, — a veritable Talleyrand, able to cope with the most distinguished statesmen among the Americans. Such of his letters as have been preserved do not suffer by comparison with the writings of even the greatest of the Americans. The most of these depended on a stately and scholarly diction to attract attention. McGillivray paid little regard to diction; but his letters possess the distinction of style, and in this particular but one American writer can be compared to him, — Benjamin Franklin. There is, in fact, a modern touch and flavor about McGillivray's letters that even the writings of Franklin do not possess. He wrote thus to Andrew Pickens, who had addressed him on behalf of the United States Government : —

"When we found that the American independence was confirmed by the peace, we expected that the new government would soon have taken some steps to make up the differences that subsisted between them and the Indians during the war, to have taken them under their protection and confirmed to them their hunting grounds. Such a course would have reconciled the minds of the Indians, and secured the States their friendship, as they considered your people their natural allies. The Georgians, whose particular interest it was to conciliate the friendship of this nation, have acted in all respects to the contrary. I am sorry to observe that violence and prejudice have taken the place of good policy and reason in all their proceedings with us. They attempted to avail themselves of our supposed distressed situation. Their talks to us breathed nothing but vengeance, and, being entirely possessed with the idea that we were wholly at their mercy, they never once reflected that colonies of a powerful monarch were nearly surrounding us, to whom, in any extremity, we might apply for succor and protection, and who, to answer some ends of their policy, might grant it to us. However, we yet deferred any such proceeding, still expecting that we could bring them to a true sense of their interest; but still finding no alteration in their conduct towards us, we sought the protection of Spain, and treaties of friendship and alliance were mutually entered into; they guaranteeing our hunting grounds and territory, and granting us a free trade in the ports of the Floridas.

" How the boundary and limits between the Spaniards and the States will be determined, a little time will show, as I believe that matter is now on foot. However, we know our limits and the extent of our hunting grounds. As a free nation, we have applied, as we had a right to do, for protection, and obtained it. We shall pay no attention to any limits that may prejudice our claims, that were drawn by an American and confirmed by a British negotiator. Yet, notwithstanding we have been obliged to adopt these measures for our preservation, and from real necessity, we sincerely wish to have it in our power to be on the same footing with the States as before the late unhappy war, to effect which is entirely in your power. We want nothing from you but justice. We want our hunting grounds preserved from encroachments. They have been ours from the beginning of time, and I trust that, with the assistance of our friends, we shall be able to maintain them against every attempt to take them from us."

Undoubtedly McGillivray was unscrupulous, and the probability is that he was mercenary; but such charges may be brought against some of the ablest men who have figured in history. When all is said, the fact remains that Alexander McGillivray was one of the most accomplished and ingenious of the politicians of his time. If he had been on the side of the whites, and had managed their interests with the skill and ability which he displayed in behalf of the Creeks, history would have written him down as a great statesman. It was only by an accidental suit at law that some of his most characteristic letters were brought to light; but those that have been rescued from oblivion show that in wielding the pen he was more than a match for the many able men who corresponded with him.

In September, 1789, Washington sent General Andrew Pickens, with three other commissioners, to treat with McGillivray. They found the great chief at Rock Landing, on the Oconee, with two thousand Creek warriors, where he had been encamped more than a week. The Indian camp was on the western bank of the river. The commissioners pitched their tents on the eastern bank. They were received by McGillivray with great courtesy. Everything progressed favorably, so much so that the commissioners read to the assembled chiefs a copy of the treaty which they had drawn up. This treaty was all in favor of the whites. The Indians were offered no equivalent for the terms proposed. It is worthy of note that Andrew Pickens wholly dissented from the terms of the proposed treaty. He knew that the Indians would have to be paid for the valuable land which the Georgians were then cultivating in the neighborhood of the Oconee, and the commissioners had been advised by the Federal authorities to pay for these lands. McGillivray broke up his encampment and retired to the Ocmulgee, nor could he be induced at that time to renew the negotiations.

President Washington was urged by the Georgia delegation in Congress to declare war against the Creeks, and this indeed was his first impulse; but when he found, from a careful estimate, that the expenses of such a war would amount to fifteen millions of dollars, he prudently gave up the idea. He took the matter in hand in a more conservative way. He appointed Colonel Marinus Willett a secret agent to visit McGillivray, and urge him to visit President Washington in New York. In this Colonel Willett was entirely successful. Accompanied by McGillivray and a number of the leading men of the Creeks, Willett set out on his return journey. At Guilford Court House, McGillivray attracted great attention on account of a very pathetic incident that occurred there some years before. A man named Brown had been killed by the Creeks, and his wife and children captured and made slaves. Their unfortunate condition came to the notice of Alexander McGillivray, and, as he had done in the case of many other captive white women and children, he paid their ransom and redeemed them from slavery. He maintained them at his house for over a year, and finally assisted them to return to their friends. Mrs. Brown, hearing that McGillivray had arrived, went to see him. At that moment he was in the courthouse, the center of a large assembly of ladies and gentlemen who had gathered to pay their respects. But this was no obstacle to Mrs. Brown. She rushed through the assembly, and, in a flood of tears, expressed her gratitude to him for saving her life and the lives of her children. She also expressed her strong admiration for his character.

In due course, McGillivray arrived in New York, where he was treated with great consideration. He had long private conferences with Washington and other officials of the government, and was finally induced to make a treaty which was satisfactory to the United States, and would have been satisfactory to Georgia if it had been carried out, but in fact the terms of it were never fulfilled. While in New York, McGillivray made a secret treaty with Washington, a fact that was not discovered for many years. It provided, that after two years from date (August, 1790) the commerce of the Creek nation should be carried on through the ports of the United States, and in the mean time through the present channels; that a number of chiefs of the Creeks and of the Seminole nation should be paid one hundred dollars a year each, and be furnished with handsome medals; that the United States should feed, clothe, and educate Creek youth at the North, not exceeding five at one time; and that Alexander McGillivray should be constituted agent of the United States, with the rank of brigadier general, and the pay of twelve hundred dollars a year. In 1792, McGillivray was a British colonel, an American brigadier general, an agent of the United States, and an agent of Spain. This extraordinary man died in Pensacola on the 17th of February, having been seized with a fatal illness while returning from one of his plantations on Little River in Putnam or Baldwin.

Another famous Creek was General William McIntosh, a half-breed. His father was Captain William McIntosh, and his mother was an Indian of unmixed blood. He was not so brilliant a man intellectually as McGillivray; but he had a native force of character, and an inborn sense of justice, that McGillivray seems to have been a stranger to. History tells us little enough of McIntosh, but that little is all to his credit. Almost from the days of Oglethorpe, there were two parties in the Creek nation, and the issue on which they divided was the treatment that should be accorded to the whites. The party division was geographical as well as political. The Upper Creeks, living upon the Alabama, Coosa, and Tallapoosa rivers, were not present at the Coweta town when James Oglethorpe treated with the Lower Creeks in August, 1730. At that time they were under the influence of the French, and afterwards they sought the protection of the Spaniards. They refused to recognize any of the treaties made by the Lower Creeks with the English, and the great body of them remained to the end the bitter enemies of the Georgians. On the other hand, the majority of the Lower Creeks were friendly with the English from the days of. Oglethorpe; and that friendship continued, with but few interruptions, down to the days of Governor Troup.

Now, McGillivray, in his day and time, represented the Upper Creeks of the Tallapoosa country and their policy, while William McIntosh represented the Lower Creeks of the Coweta country and their policy. The division in the Creek nation was so serious, that, when the Upper Creeks took sides with the British in the War of 1812, they found themselves opposed in the field by a large party of Lower Creeks under the command of McIntosh. Thus, at the battle of Autossee, William McIntosh led a large band of Lower Creeks against those who were making war on the whites. He made himself so conspicuous in that affair, that General Floyd mentions him in the official report of the battle.

The treaty at Indian Spring, and the results that followed, cannot be clearly understood unless we bear in mind the political differences that existed between the Upper and the Lower Creeks. The Creek chiefs and the commissioners met at Indian Spring on the 15th of February, 1825. The chiefs and warriors of the Upper Creeks declared that no treaty could be made for a cession of lands, and on the night of the 11th they went home. On the 12th a treaty was signed with the McIntosh party. Colonel John A. Crowell, agent for the Creek Indians, sent a letter to the secretary of war, in which he declared that the treaty was in direct opposition to the letter and spirit of the instructions to the commissioners; but the treaty was sent to Washington, and was ratified on the 3d of March, 1825. When the Indians of the Upper Creeks and their party learned that the treaty had been ratified, they became very much excited. McIntosh and his party went to Milledgeville, and told the governor that they expected violent treatment at the hands of the Upper Creeks. They begged the protection of the State and of the United States, and this was promised them.

STO. OF GA. — 14

Out of this treaty grew a very serious conflict between the Federal and State governments. After a good deal of discussion, the President asked Congress to reconsider the treaty of Indian Spring, and presented a new one as a substitute, which was ratified and proclaimed; but popular indignation ran so high in Georgia, that Governor Troup felt justified in paying no attention to this new treaty. He proceeded to carry out the terms of the Indian Spring treaty. Charges were brought against Crowell, the Indian agent. The governor informed T. P. Andrews, the special agent, that he would hold no further correspondence with him. The conduct of General Gaines had been such that Governor Troup requested the Federal Government to recall, arrest, and punish him. In 1826 the State Legislature declared that the attempt to repeal the treaty of Indian Spring by the substitution of another treaty was illegal and unconstitutional. In September, 1826, Governor Troup ordered the districts ceded by the treaty of Indian Spring to be surveyed. When the Indians complained of this, the secretary of war wrote to Governor Troup that the President felt himself compelled to employ all the means under his control to maintain the faith of the nation by carrying the treaty into effect, meaning the treaty made at Washington, and intended to be a substitute for the Indian Spring treaty. In his reply, Governor Troup declared that he would feel it to be his duty to resist to the utmost any military attack which the President of the United States should think proper to make upon the Territory, the people, or the sovereignty of Georgia. " From the first deci-

sive act of hostility," he wrote to the secretary of war,
"you will be considered and treated as a public enemy.
You have referred me, as the rule ot my conduct, to
the treaty of Washington. In turn I refer you to the
treaty of prior date and prior ratification, concluded at
the Indian Spring."

The President issued orders that the surveyors appointed by the State be prosecuted. Governor Troup
thereupon ordered the proper officers, in every instance
of complaint made of the arrest of any surveyor, to
take all necessary and legal measures to effect their
liberation, and to bring to justice all the parties concerned in such arrests, as violators of the peace and
personal security of the State. He also ordered the
major generals of the militia to hold the various regiments and battalions in readiness to repel any hostile
invasion of the State. But no acts of violence were
committed. The surveyors were not arrested, the sur-
veys were made, and the lands ceded by the treaty of
Indian Spring were divided by lottery in 1827.

The Upper Creeks, who had always been unfriendly
to the Georgians, were so angry at the signing of the
treaty of Indian Spring, that they determined to assassinate General William McIntosh. They had never for-
given him for leading his party of Lower Creeks against
them in the campaign that was made necessary by the
terrible massacre of Fort Mims, and they now determined to rid themselves of him at once and forever.

We have seen that General McIntosh, and his party
of Lower Creeks, suspecting that an attack would be
made on them by the powerful tribes on the Talla-

poosa, went to Milledgeville to beg the governor to protect them. Protection was promised, but never given. Meanwhile the Upper Creeks held a secret council, and selected a hundred and seventy of the boldest warriors in the nation to murder McIntosh. They marched in the most cautious way. They reached the neighborhood of McIntosh's home, and concealed themselves, to wait for night to fall. About sundown, or a little before, the Indians saw from their hiding place two persons riding along a trail. One was McIntosh, and the other a man named Hawkins, who had married one of McIntosh's daughters. It would have been an easy matter for the savages to have killed McIntosh at this time; but they had made up their minds to kill him upon his own premises, so that his blood might stain the land that had been granted him by the State. While still in sight of the men who had been sent to slay him, McIntosh bade Hawkins good evening, wheeled his horse, and rode back on the trail toward his home. Although he was now alone, the Indians would not kill him. They had fixed up a different plan, and they carried it out.

Before dark the Indians gathered together a supply of "fat lightwood," as the resinous pine was called. This they split into convenient length, and made up into three bundles to be carried on the backs of their warriors. They remained hidden within half a mile of McIntosh's house till three o'clock in the morning, and then silently and swiftly marched to the place. They had taken along with them a man named James Hutton to act as interpreter, the reason for this being that McIntosh was in the habit of entertaining travelers.

It was to be Hutton's duty to assure such as might be found there that they would not be disturbed in any manner. Guests of McIntosh were commonly lodged in an outhouse in the yard; and Hutton, accompanied by two Indians, went to this building to see who might be sleeping there. They found a peddler in one bed, and Chilly, a son of General McIntosh, in another.

Young McIntosh, as if instinctively understanding the nature of the visit, sprang from the bed and leaped out at a window. He was fired upon by the Indians, but was not touched, and succeeded in making his escape. The peddler was nearly scared out of his wits;

but his pack of goods was removed to a place of safety, and the house in which he had been sleeping was soon in flames.

Meanwhile most of the Indians had surrounded McIntosh's house, and torches of the fat pine were used to set it on fire. The red men danced around the burning building, yelling, and crying out, " McIntosh, we have come, we have come! We told you if you sold the land to the Georgians we would come. Now we have come!" At the first alarm McIntosh had barricaded his front door. He stood near it; and when it was broken down, he fired upon his assailants. At that moment, one of his firmest friends, Toma Tustenuggee, who had thrown himself upon the party at the door, fell on the threshold, riddled with bullets. General McIntosh then retreated to the second story with four guns, which he continued to fire from the windows.

The flames drove him from the second story to the first floor again. He fought bravely to the end, but was soon compelled to expose himself to the fire of his enemies. He fell to the floor, pierced by many bullets, and was dragged into the yard by his heels. He breathed defiance to the last, and was finally stabbed to death. After this savage deed, the Indians plundered the houses, killed such cattle as they could find, and committed other outrages. A small party of the Indians had followed Hawkins the evening before. His house was surrounded about daybreak the next morning, and he was ordered to come out. He refused, and defended himself the best he could; but he was finally taken prisoner and tied, until the fate of McIntosh was known. Then he was murdered, and his body thrown into the river near where he lived. The Indians marched back to the Tallapoosa country with the scalps of these unfortunate men. McIntosh's scalp was suspended from a pole in the public square of Ocfuskee, and young and old danced around it with shouts of joy.

General McIntosh was a cousin of Governor Troup, being the son of Governor Troup's uncle, Captain William McIntosh, who was frequently on the Chattahoochee before the breaking-out of the Revolution.

REMOVAL OF THE CHEROKEES.

WHEN Georgia had begun to recover its breath, after the difficulties with the Creeks, the people had time to discover that they had a much more serious problem to deal with in the Cherokee nation, which occupied all the northwestern portion of the State. Those who mingled thrift with their benevolence, and had the courage to think about the future of the whites as well as the future of the savages, thought that both ends would be attained by making a permanent settlement for the Indians beyond the Mississippi River. Those whose benevolence was a mixture of sentimentality and romantic misinformation thought the Indians ought to be left where contact with the whites would tend to civilize and Christianize them. Consequently there were two parties to the discussion, and a good deal of practical selfishness at the bottom of it all. There used to be an old song running in this wise,—

> "All I want in this creation,
> Is a pretty little wife and a big plantation
> Away up yonder in the Cherokee nation,"—

and this song no doubt represented the real feeling behind the whole matter. The big plantation was what was really wanted. At the same time it should not be forgotten that it was for the benefit of the Indians as well as the whites that they should be settled in a section where they would remain undisturbed. This policy has been proven by time to be the true one.

Travelers and romancers have done no end of harm by exalting the Indian character, covering up its faults, and exaggerating its merits. Romance has made great heroes of the Indians; but in the whole history of the red men, so far as it has been faithfully chronicled, the names of the Indians of unmixed blood who are worth remembering can be counted on the fingers of two hands.

Sequoia, or George Guess, who invented the Cherokee alphabet, was the grandson of a white man. This invention, however, was a very remarkable achievement, and it is worthy of a word here. Sequoia was altogether illiterate. He could neither write nor speak English, but he saw that the whites could talk with each other by means of pieces of paper. So he set himself to work to examine his own language. He found that sixty monosyllables could be so combined as to represent every word in the Cherokee language, and for each of these syllables he formed a character. Many of these characters were taken from an English spelling book which he managed to get hold of. Some are Greek characters, and others are letters of the English alphabet turned upside down; but each character in the Cherokee alphabet stands for a monosyllable. It happened, too, from the structure of the Cherokee language or dialect, that the syllabic alphabet is also in the nature of a grammar; so that those who know the language by ear, and master the alphabet, can at once read and write. Owing to the extreme simplicity of this system, it can be acquired in a few days. Some have learned it even in one day. Thus it happened that the Cherokees, who were at the beginning of one year ignorant and illiterate, had become in the course of a few months able to read and write their own language. They accomplished this without going to school, and without expense of time or money.

This curious and useful invention is dwelt on here because it stands alone. The Indian grandson of a white man remains to-day the only man, in the long history of the aborigines, who has done anything for the real and lasting benefit of his race.

When the people of Georgia insisted on the removal of that nation to the Far West, the Cherokees were neither better nor worse than the rest of the Indians. Some of the half-breeds had indeed begun to put on the airs of civilization, and many of them had put off their barbarian garbs; but from time to time they gave evidence that contact with the whites had only whetted their savage appetites for cruelty. The Indian in Cooper's novels and the Indian in real life are two different creatures. They were tall and straight because they refused to do manual labor. The drudgery was left to the women, who hoed the corn when at home, and carried the burdens when the warriors were moving about. They cultivated the passion of revenge. Those who know them best have declared in a thousand ways that they never found in the red men any solid, substantial, or agreeable quality. They were brave, but so is a bulldog.

There is no wonder that Georgia wanted to get rid of them as neighbors. The people showed their anxiety in this matter when, in 1802, they conveyed to the United States Government all the valuable lands that now form the States of Alabama and Mississippi; the consideration being that the General Government would secure from the Indians, and open up to settlement, the lands which they then held in the State. In 1808 the Cherokees asked the United States to allow them to examine the public land west of the Mississippi, and, if pleased, to settle on it. Permission was given, and the Cherokees sent a party to explore the lands. The country suited them so well that many of the Indians emigrated at once. The General Government thus had an opportunity to carry out the contract of 1802, but failed to do so. It had another opportunity in 1814, when the conquered Creeks sued for peace. The General Government had the right to demand of them the cession of the land they occupied in Georgia. Instead, it took land in Alabama, which it sold for its own benefit.

And so the matter went on from year to year, and the people waited patiently; for they had become aware, from costly experience, that one of the prices they have to pay for popular government is the occasional rule of the political demagogue.

In 1827, when the people of Georgia began to grow restive under the failure of the government to carry out its contracts, the Cherokees had declared themselves to be an independent state. They had their own printed constitution and code of laws. So that

here in the limits of Georgia there were three governments going on at one and the same time. The
United States prohibited any person from settling on
Indian territory, or trading with any Indian, without a
special license from the proper authority. In addition
to this, the State of Georgia had found it necessary to
extend her criminal courts over the Cherokee territory,
in order to protect her own citizens.

The half-breeds among the Cherokees were very
shrewd and unscrupulous. They had caused some of
their tribe to take possession of lands ceded to Georgia
by the Creeks, and in this way sought to add confusion
to the discussion that was then going on. The Indians
took possession by force. They were armed and
painted, and led by Chief Ridge. Fourteen or fifteen
houses were burned by these savages, and the white
women and children were left exposed to the weather,
the ground being covered with snow.

The great trouble with the Cherokees then and afterwards was, that the government of their nation had
fallen into the hands of half-breeds, whose education
only gave them fresh opportunities to gain wealth and
power at the expense of the rest of the tribe. They
owned trading houses, big plantations, numbers of
slaves, had charge of the ferries, and controlled all the
traffic between the whites and the Indians. As these
half-breeds became wealthier, the rest of the tribe
became poorer. They had forsaken their primitive
habits and customs, and taken up those of the most
depraved whites who lived among them. It is worthy
of note that the most progressive spirits among the

Cherokees were in favor of emigration beyond the Mississippi. The leaders of this party were natives of
unmixed blood, who saw that the control of the corrupt
half-breeds was carrying the nation to ruin. Several of
these leaders were waylaid and shot down by the agents
of those whose policy they were opposing. The alarm
in some sections was very great. The citizens met, and
adopted resolutions requesting the government to station
troops at suitable points, for the protection of the lives
and property of the whites and friendly Indians.

Under an act of the Legislature, a body of militia
had been organized, under the name of the "Georgia
Guard." It was the duty of the Guard to protect the
citizens of Georgia and the friendly Cherokees. John
Howard Payne, the famous author of " Home, Sweet
Home," was arrested by this Guard. The poet was
traveling among the Cherokees for information, and
was no doubt ignorant of the state of feeling then exist-
ing. He was finally suspected by the vigilant Georgia
Guard of writing improper papers. He had been seen
making notes, and when he was arrested his papers
were searched. The commander of the Georgia Guard,
Colonel William N. Bishop, reported to the governor
that he had examined some of Mr. Payne's papers, and
found some very improper and indiscreet statements
about the President, the government, and the State
authorities, and many bitter remarks concerning
Cherokee matters. Evidently, Colonel Bishop was of
the opinion, that, while a politician or a newspaper
editor might be allowed to indulge in improper and
indiscreet statements about Presidents and other public

men, a poet had no such rights. But the colonel finally discharged Mr. Payne from custody, and the very foolish proceeding was condemned by a resolution of the General Assembly.

In 1835 two parties had developed in the Cherokee nation. One was in favor of removal to the Western lands, and the other was opposed to removal. John Ridge headed the removal party, and John Ross the opposition. In February of that year these men went to Washington at the head of deputations, and entered into negotiations with the General Government. After a great deal of talk, excitement, confusion, and trouble, the Cherokee people finally concluded to hold a meeting at Red Clay in October, 1835. There was a good deal of angry feeling between those of the Cherokees who were in favor of a treaty of removal and those who were opposed to it. Major Ridge, John Ridge, and David Vann were impeached for holding opinions contrary to those held by the Cherokee authorities. On the other hand, many of those in favor of removal met, and passed resolutions, in which they declared that their people could not prosper in the midst of a white population, and that, while they loved the lands of their fathers, and would leave the place of their birth with regret, they considered that it would be better to become exiles than to submit to the laws of the State.

At the Red Clay meeting, arrangements were made for discussing with the United States authorities the terms of a treaty of removal. The Ross party was still violently opposed to removal. John Ross, the leader of this party, was only one fourth Indian, the other three fourths being Scotch and American. Ross was very shrewd and thrifty, and had accumulated a great deal of property, with the prospect of accumulating more. He had many sympathizers and admirers in all parts of the country. It seems to have been thought a wonderful thing in that day, that a man one quarter Indian should be able to read and write English, and make political speeches. When everything had been arranged for the final treaty, and while negotiations were going forward, Ross and his party put an end to them, and went to Washington, where they hoped to delay matters. But the Ridge party met the United States commissioners at New Echota on the 21st of December, 1835, according to appointment, and on the 29th the treaty was concluded. On May 23, 1836, it was ratified.

By the terms of this treaty, the Cherokees, in consideration of the sum of five million dollars, relinquished all claims to lands east of the Mississippi. In addition to the money to be paid, they were to receive seven million acres of land west of the Mississippi. Should this territory be found to be insufficient, the United States, in consideration of five hundred thousand dollars, was to convey to them an additional body of land. The land thus granted was not to be included within the limits of any State at any future time. The Cherokees were guaranteed protection against domestic strife and foreign enemies, and it was provided that the tribe should be entitled to a delegate in the House of Representatives whenever

Congress passed a law to that effect. The United
States authorities were to remove the Cherokees to
their new homes, and to provide for their support
for one year after they were settled. There were
other provisions, all in favor of the Cherokees. The
Indians were to be removed within two years after
the ratification of the treaty.

Ross, and other leaders opposed to removal, had gone
to Washington. While there they were informed, by
Major Ridge and others, of the treaty at New Echota.
Ross refused to make any reply to the communication,
but tried to make a new treaty. He was told that he
could not be received to make a new treaty. The attitude of the Ross party, together with certain threats
that had been made by their followers, led many citizens of Georgia to believe that the Indians opposed
to removal would, in accordance with their character
and history, revenge themselves by making night
attacks on the unprotected people. Consequently
those most likely to be the victims of such attacks
petitioned the governor for arms, ammunition, and
troops; and these petitions were granted. A battalion
of militia was raised, and placed at Lashley's Ferry
on the Coosa River, with orders to keep the Cherokees in check, and also to prevent the Creeks from
coming into Georgia. Many of the Cherokees were
disarmed; and five hundred muskets, with ammunition,
were sent into Cherokee County, for the use of the
people in the event of any hostile movement on the
part of the Indians.

The State of Georgia was to take possession of the

territory ceded by the treaty on the twenty-fourth day
of May, 1838, and the military were got in readiness for
removing the Indians. General Scott, of the United
States army, called on the governor of Georgia for two
regiments, and to this call there was a prompt response.
By the 18th of May enough men had arrived at New
Echota, where the troops were to assemble, to organize
a regiment; and on the morning of the 24th the troops
took up the line of march for the purpose of collecting
the Indians. This continued until the 3d of June,
when the troops and the Indians started for Ross's
Landing on the Tennessee River. About fifteen hundred Indians had been collected by the Georgia troops,
and these troops were then dismissed from the service
of the United States.

The rest of the work was done by the regular army,
which, being divided into small detachments, went about
the Cherokee country, making prisoners of family after
family, and carrying them to the camps. The most
careful arrangements had been made to prevent cruelty
or disorder, and there has never been any complaint
as to the manner in which the troops performed their
duty. Nearly the whole nation had been gathered into
camps by the end of June. At that time some of
the Indians began their march to the West; but the
great body of the tribe, fourteen thousand in number,
did not begin their westward journey until September,
owing to the hot weather. Every arrangement that
could be suggested was made for the comfort of the
Indians in their march; but from May, when the
removal began, to the time when the last company

STO. OF GA. — 15

had completed its journey, more than four thousand persons died.

One year afterwards, on the 22d of June, 1839, Major Ridge, John Ridge, and Elias Boudinot, all of whom had taken an active part in negotiating the treaty of removal, were assassinated.

Since their removal the Cherokees have prospered to a greater extent than any other Indian tribe. They have a government of their own, flourishing schools, and books and newspapers printed in their own language. It is the only tribe of American Indians that has shown any desire or ability to share in the benefits of civilization.

THE BEGINNING OF PARTIES IN GEORGIA.

THE first serious political division in Georgia after the Revolution had a very curious beginning. There is always, of course, a division among the people on great public questions as they arise. But the War of the Revolution had so solidified public sentiment that nothing occurred to jar it until the Yazoo Fraud created some division. Even then public sentiment was so overwhelmingly opposed to the sale of the lands to the speculators, that the few who favored it were not numerous nor respectable enough to be called a party.

On the 24th of February, 1806, Mr. Josiah Glass, having come all the way from North Carolina in search of a Mr. Robert Clary, went to the town of Sparta with a warrant which he requested Judge Charles Tait to indorse. This Judge Tait did in due form. The warrant was for negro stealing, and was directed against Mr. Robert Clary. Mr. Clary was arrested by Mr. Josiah Glass in Washington County, and was carried to Greene County Superior Court. On the first day of the court, Mr. Josiah Glass wrote a letter to Judge Tait, and requested him to attend, and take the examination of a man then in his custody, who would make confessions highly interesting to the State and the United

States. Judge Tait, accompanied by Squire Oliver Skinner, attended that night, and took a part of the confessions of Mr. Robert Clary, and completed them the following night. Then he gave Mr. Josiah Glass a certified copy of the same to take with him to North Carolina, to which State he was taking Mr. Robert Clary, on a warrant charging him with negro stealing.

Now, it seems that the warrant against Clary was merely intended as a scheme to get him to North Carolina to testify against a man named Collins. History has suppressed the confessions made by Mr. Robert Clary; but it is certain that they contained a most offensive charge against General John Clarke, whose patriotic services in behalf of the people during the Revolution gave him great fame and popularity. No sooner did John Clarke hear of this affair than he proceeded to act with his usual promptness. When he learned the particulars about the taking of the affidavit at night, he at once jumped to the conclusion that he had been made the victim of a conspiracy. There had been some disagreement between him and Hon. William H. Crawford; and as Judge Tait had been the partner of

Mr. Crawford, and was his firm friend, — for Crawford was a man great enough to command and deserve friends, — General Clarke suspected that Clary and Glass had been made tools of to damage his reputation.

General Clarke acted at once. He presented a memorial to the Legislature, making certain charges against Judge Tait with respect to the taking of the "dark-lantern affidavits," as they were called by his friends. The Legislature found, as it ought to have done, that the charges made in the memorial of General Clarke were unsupported by fact or evidence. In the very nature of things, it could not be shown that an honorable judge of the Superior Court of Georgia, in certifying to an affidavit containing the confession of a mere adventurer, was engaged in a conspiracy; but the question with which General Clarke had to deal was, how did the offensive and malicious matter, contained in an affidavit taken by a judge and one witness at night, become public property? If General Clarke had been a more thoroughgoing politician, he would have found a better way to confound his enemies than that which he adopted; but he was deeply wounded by a foul charge made at night, and put in circulation by means of nods and winks and whispers. His first recourse was to the Legislature, consequently it had the effect of strengthening both his friends and his enemies. His friends were indignant at the action of the Legislature. His enemies professed to be astonished that arrogance should fly so high as to bring before the Legislature unfounded charges against a judge of the superior courts.

The legislative record is not as full as it might be. There was something behind the Clary business that does not appear on the records of the House and Senate. General Clarke wrote a pamphlet entitled "A Legacy for My Children," in which, according to Judge Garnett Andrews (see " Reminiscences of an Old Georgia Lawyer"), the matter of his memorial to the Legislature is differently stated. According to Judge Andrews, who bases his authority on General Clarke's pamphlet and on the testimony of those who were familiar with the facts, Clary was arrested and carried before Judge Tait on a charge of stealing horses. Clary charged General Clarke with complicity. Mr. Crawford was the prosecuting attorney. General Clarke accused Judge Tait and Mr. Crawford with instigating Clary to make the charge.

The truth seems to be, that Clary, knowing the differences that existed between these distinguished men, sought to help his own case by making the charge against General Clarke, and that the latter was quite ready to believe that his two opponents had originated the charges for the purpose of doing him a mortal injury. Feeling assured of the justice of his cause, he appealed to the Legislature. This failing, he took the matter into his own hands. He challenged Mr. Crawford, shot him through the wrist, and then challenged him again. A little later, cantering along a street in Milledgeville on his fine sorrel horse, General Clarke saw Judge Tait before him in a sulky. He spurred his horse forward, and laid his whip across the judge's shoulders two or three times.

These events created great excitement throughout the State. There had already been controversy and division caused by the duel between Mr. Crawford and Van Allen, a cousin of President Van Buren, and at that time attorney-general of the State. Van Allen was killed ; and there was a great controversy in Georgia, in consequence, as to who was right and who was wrong. This excitement became furious in the course

of the contest between Clarke and Crawford. Crawford was fortunately lifted out of it by being made a United States senator in 1807. His distinguished career afterwards is well known. He was minister to France, secretary of the treasury, Vice-President of the United States, and would have been elected President but for reports circulated throughout the country that he had been stricken down with a fatal illness.

But the contest between the Clarke and Crawford par-

ties continued to rage. Whatever issue the Clarke men
were favorable to, the Crawford men opposed. Whatever scheme the Clarke men suggested, the Crawford
men fought. There was nothing polite about the contest. People who wore gloves pulled them off. In
cold weather the voters were warm, and in hot weather
they were steaming. The contest went on before
elections, and was kept up with just as much energy
after elections. No vote could settle it, and no success could quiet it. It was in the nature of a political squabble, covering the whole State, dividing districts,
counties, cities, towns, villages, settlements, beats, cross-
roads groceries, and families. It was a knock-down-
and-drag-out fight, in which hair pulling, gouging, and
biting were allowed.

While Crawford was advancing step by step in
national politics, his party in Georgia took up George
M. Troup, one of the most brilliant and aggressive
men in the State. The contest had been going on
for twenty years when Troup came upon the scene,
in 1830, as a candidate for governor. He had been
a member of the State Legislature, a representative in
Congress, and a United States senator: therefore in
1820, when he was nominated for governor by the
Crawford party, he was ripe in experience. He was
forty years old, and full of the fire and energy that
marked his whole career. The Crawford party now
became the Troup party, and the contests that followed were the most exciting that ever took place in
the State before, or that have ever taken place since.

At that time the General Assembly elected the governor, the people selecting members favorable to the candidates they preferred. As the result of the first campaign between the Clarke and Troup parties, General John Clarke was elected by a majority of thirteen legislative votes. When Governor Clarke's term expired, he was again opposed by Troup, and was again elected, but this time by a majority of only two legislative votes. In 1823, Matthew Talbot represented the Clarke party, but was defeated by Troup. In 1825, General Clarke again entered the contest. The election was no longer in the hands of the Legislature, but was by popular vote. Governor Troup's treatment of the Indian question, and the firm stand he had taken in favor of the rights of the State, had materially increased his influence, and he was elected over Clarke by a majority of 683 votes.

Curious to relate, the old Clarke party became the Union party, and in 1840 was the Democratic party. The Crawford party became the States Rights party, and in 1840 was the Whig party. Such was the evolution of parties in Georgia.

A QUEER CASE.

A VERY queer, not to say mysterious case, was brought to trial in Jones County in 1837, at the April term of the Superior Court. It has had no parallel in Georgia before or since, and had none in any other country, so far as the present writer is aware, until the celebrated Tichborne case was brought to trial in England a few years ago. The Bunkley case created quite as much excitement, and caused quite as much division in public opinion in Georgia, as the Tichborne case did in England.

Jesse L. Bunkley belonged to a good family in Jones County, and when he came of age would have fallen heir to an estate worth forty thousand dollars. An effort was made to give him all the advantages

of education, but these he refused to accept. He
was a wild boy, and was fonder of wild company
than of his books. He went to school for a while
in Eatonton, but got into some scrape there and ran
away. He was afterwards sent to Franklin College,
now the State University, where he entered the grammar school. Such discipline as they had in those days
was irksome to young Bunkley, and he soon grew tired
of it. He left the college, and, after roving about for
a while, returned to his home in Jones County. In
his twentieth year, 1825, being well supplied with
money, he left his home for the purpose of traveling.
He went to the Southwest, and in that year wrote to
his mother from New Orleans.

No other letter was received from him during that
year or the next, and in 1827 word was brought to
Jones County that Jesse Bunkley was dead. The
rumor, for it seems to have been nothing more, was
regarded by the family as true. At any rate, no
attempt was made to investigate it. Jesse was the
black sheep of the family; he had been away from
home a good deal; his conduct when at home had
not been such as to commend him to the affections
of his people; and his mother had married a third
husband, a man named Lowther: consequently the
vague news of the young man's death was probably
received with a feeling of relief. There was always a
probability that such a wild and dissipated youngster
would come to some bad end; but with his death that
probability ceased to be even a possibility, and so, no
doubt with a sigh of relief, young Bunkley's people

put aside the memory of him. He was dead and buried. Those who survived him were more than willing to take the care and trouble of managing the estate which young Bunkley would have inherited had he returned and claimed it.

But in 1833, Major Smith of Jones County received a letter purporting to be from Jesse L. Bunkley, and it related to matters that both Smith and Bunkley were familiar with. In December, 1833, Mrs. Lowther, his mother, received a letter from a person claiming to be her son Jesse. The letter was dated at the New Orleans prison. It appears from this letter that the family of Bunkley had already taken steps to disown the person who had written to Major Smith, and who claimed to be Jesse Bunkley. The letter to Mrs. Lowther was very awkwardly written. It was misspelled, and bore no marks of punctuation; and yet it is just such a letter as might be written by a man who took no interest in his books when a schoolboy, and had had no occasion to look into them or to handle a pen. He said in this letter that he wrote to convince his mother that he was her own child, though it appeared that she wished to disown him. This, he declared in his awkward way, he knew no reason for, unless it was on account of his past folly. He then went on to relate some facts about the family and his own school days. The mother did not answer this letter, because, as she said afterwards on the witness stand, she did not consider that it was from her son. She was satisfied, she said, that the letter was not in her son's handwriting.

The person claiming to be Jesse L. Bunkley reached Jones County some time afterwards. His case, in the nature of things, excited great public interest. Hundreds of people who had known Jesse recognized him in this claimant. On the other hand, hundreds who had also known Bunkley when a boy failed to recognize him in the claimant. Meanwhile those who had charge of the Bunkley property took prompt action. They went before the grand jury, and had the claimant indicted for cheating and swindling; and thus began the celebrated case of the State against Elijah Barber, *alias* Jesse L. Bunkley.

The claimant came to Jones County in 1836, was indicted in that year, and his case was brought to trial in the Superior Court in April, 1837. A great deal of time was taken up in the investigation. More than one hundred and thirty witnesses were examined. Ninety-eight, the majority of these being disinterested persons, declared that they believed the claimant to be an impostor. More than forty disinterested persons declared under oath that they believed the claimant to be Jesse L. Bunkley, and the majority of these last witnesses had known Bunkley long and intimately.

The efforts of the prosecution were directed to showing that the man claiming to be Jesse Bunkley was in reality Elijah Barber, who in 1824–25 was a wagoner who hauled lumber from Grace's Mill near Macon, who was also known in Upson County, and who had served in the Florida war. Some of the witnesses who had never known Bunkley recognized the claimant as a man who had called himself Barber. Some of the witnesses

who had known Jesse from his boyhood testified that they recognized the claimant as Bunkley on sight. Bunkley had various scars on his face, neck, and body. The claimant exhibited all these to the jury. One of the witnesses remembered that Bunkley bore the marks of a snake bite on one of his legs. The claimant immediately showed these marks. Hundreds of questions had been put to the claimant to test his memory. A great many he answered correctly, a great many others he failed to answer; but his replies to all vital questions were wonderfully clear and satisfactory. The jury was out but a short time before it returned, bringing in a verdict of guilty; and the claimant was sentenced to the penitentiary, where he served out his term.

This verdict and sentence settled the case in law, but it remained as unsettled as ever in the public mind. The writer of this has heard it discussed on more than one occasion among old ladies and gentlemen who knew Bunkley, and who saw the claimant; and, without exception, they declared that the verdict of the jury was cruelly unjust.

And yet, if any wrong was done, Bunkley himself was to blame for it. Being a young man of fortune and of the fairest prospects, he owed it to himself, his family, his friends, and to society at large, to become a good citizen, so that his ample means might be properly employed. Instead of that, he became a rowdy and a rioter, spending his days and his nights in evil company and in dissipation. If the claimant in this mysterious case was really Jesse Bunkley, it may be said of him that his sins had found him out.

GEORGIA WIT AND HUMOR.

THE wit and humor of Georgia stand by themselves. They have no counterpart in any other section of the country. Many attempts have been made to imitate them, but there is always something lacking. The flavor, the "bouquet," the aroma, is gone. The sun, the soil, the air, and even the spring water, seem to have something to do with it. Just what, nobody knows. Wit and humor are elusive, — they are unsubstantial. On the other hand, the Georgia watermelon is something solid. It may be handled and felt. It may be "thumped" and "plugged" and tested. Those who know what a watermelon is and should be, know that there is none to compare with the melons that are grown in Georgia, no matter what the variety. The same may be said of the wit and humor that belong to Georgia. An old man — Uncle Tom Norris he was called, on account of his gray hairs — was once heard to say (speaking professionally), "Let me clap a drop of the low-wines to my tongue, and I'll tell you what branch the fire was kindled on." He was a distiller, and knew his business. One need not be an expert to say the same of Georgia humor. It is almost possible to tell the very militia district in which it originated. It carries not only the flavor, but the color.

For a hundred years Georgia has remained the most democratic part of the country. The sons of the richest men were put in the fields to work side by side with the negroes, and were thus taught to understand the importance of individual effort that leads to personal independence. It thus happened that there was a cordial, and even an affectionate, understanding between the slaves and their owners, that perhaps had no parallel elsewhere. The poorer whites had no reason to hold their heads down because they had to work for their living. The richest slave owners did not feel themselves above those who had few negroes or none. When a man called his neighbor " Colonel," or " Judge," it was to show his respect, nothing more. For the rest, the humblest held their heads as high as the richest, and were as quick, perhaps quicker, in a quarrel.

The Virginians and North Carolinians who settled in the Broad River region intermarried, and spread out over middle Georgia. Those who were not akin were bound to each other by ties of long acquaintanceship; but the homogeneousness of the people, complete and thorough as it was, was not marked by any monotony. On the contrary, character and individuality ran riot, appearing in such strange and attractive shapes as to puzzle and bewilder even those who were familiar with the queer manifestations. Every settlement had its peculiarities, and every neighborhood boasted of its humorist, — its clown, whose pranks and jests were limited by no license. Out of this has grown a literature which, in some of its characteristics, is not matched elsewhere on the globe; but that which has been preserved by printing is not comparable, either in volume or merit, with the great body of humor that has perished because of the lack of some one industrious enough to chronicle it.

One of the most perfect types of the Georgia humorist was the late John M. Dooly. Judge Dooly was a remarkable man in other respects, but it is his wonderful fund of humor that has made his name famous in Georgia and throughout the country. It has been told in these pages how Colonel John Dooly was dragged from his bed by the Tories and murdered. This Colonel Dooly was the father of John M., who was hid under the bed when the Tories dragged his father out and murdered him. It might be supposed that such an event would have a tendency to give a boy a very serious view of life. Judge Dooly's views were no doubt serious enough ; but they were overwhelmed and overpowered by a temperament which found cause for laughter in almost every person and passing event, and was the cause of innocent mirth in others.

Judge Dooly was born in what he called the " Dark Corner " of Lincoln County, which had not then been cut off from Wilkes. After the murder of his father, the family was left in poverty. When he went to Washington, the county seat of Wilkes County, to read law with Mr. Matthews, the clothes he wore were in such a condition that he was compelled to confine himself to the office in the daytime. He was very poor and very bright. Old people who knew him when a boy, described him to Judge Garnett Andrews as " a sallow, piney-woods-looking lad." " Piney-woods people " was the local name for the tackies, the clay eaters, the no-accounts, that had settled about on the poorer lands in that section of Georgia, and given themselves over to thriftlessness for good and all. But young Dooly had that within him which made him superior to the conditions and limitations of poverty. Apart from his remarkable gift of humor, he had a native brilliancy of mind that gave him an easy mastery over the principles of law that he found in the books. He was admitted to the bar in 1798, and was immediately successful as a lawyer. His education had been limited to that which he found in the " old field schools," and in that day they were not of the best; but such a mind as his needed only the rudiments, the rest came as by instinct.

Judge Dooly was not a student while practicing at the bar. He had thoroughly mastered the principles, the groundwork, of the law; and his mind, as logical as it was brilliant, fitted these principles to every case he had charge of. His love of humor, and his fondness for the society of those who preferred fun and frolic, placed many temptations in his way, and some of these he did not always resist; but the faults he had were the faults of the time in which he lived, the faults of the society in which he was brought up and by which he was surrounded. Judge Dooly has been described by a contemporary as having a large head, with a bold, high forehead, heavy eyebrows, prominent nose, a small compressed mouth, and large, vivid, sparkling eyes, which, when the spirit of humor had possession of him, illuminated his countenance as if an electric battery were in play.

On one occasion, Judge Dooly had been challenged by Judge Tait, — the same Judge Tait who had made himself so obnoxious to General John Clarke. Judge Tait had a wooden leg; and Judge Dooly, in replying to the challenge, referred to this fact, and said he did not think they could fight on equal terms. He hoped his refusal would not be interpreted as a reflection on the misfortunes of Judge Tait. This reply made Judge Tait more indignant than ever. He wrote a severe reply, suggesting to Judge Dooly that his refusal to fight was the result of cowardice rather than a desire not to shed the blood of an unfortunate cripple. In answer to this insinuation, Judge Dooly declared boldly that he was ready to fight his adversary on anything like equal terms. He announced that he would meet Judge Tait anywhere, on any day, and exchange a shot with him, provided he (Judge Dooly) was allowed to stand on the field of honor with one leg in a bee-gum! The bee-gums of that day were made of sections of hollow trees. Naturally this remarkable proposition made Judge Tait madder than ever, and he wrote to Judge Dooly that he intended to publish him as a coward. Judge Dooly calmly informed Judge Tait by letter that he had no sort of objection to the publication, provided it was at Tait's expense. He declared, that, for his part, he would rather fill a dozen newspapers than one coffin. These unexpected strokes of humor disarmed the anger of Judge Tait, and set the whole State in a roar. They did more : they cleared the political atmosphere, and took the edge off of party rancor, which was at that time very fierce and keen.

Once, when dining at a public table, Dooly said something or did something to irritate Major Freeman Walker. The latter, remarking that he had borne with the liberties taken by Judge Dooly quite long enough, said he proposed to resent them then and there. The attack on his feelings had been made in public, and he proposed to resent it in public. Seizing a chair, he advanced on Judge Dooly. The judge seized a carving knife, and braced himself for defense. Several gentlemen caught hold of the judge to prevent him from using the knife, while only one held Major Walker. Surveying the scene, Judge Dooly calmly remarked, "Gentlemen, one of you will be sufficient to prevent me from doing any mischief. The rest of you had better hold Walker." The explosion that this remark created put even Major Walker in good humor, and he and the judge settled their differences in the most amiable and rational manner.

When the Legislature passed severe laws against gaming, Judge Dooly enforced them rigidly. Some of the gamblers were brought to trial and fined, and others were only saved from arrest by the fact that they kept out of the way when court was in session.

But one night in Washington, Wilkes County, after the judge had been holding court all the week and had closed the term, he went to his room in the hotel and made all preparations to retire. He had barely settled himself in bed, when he heard a noise in an adjoining room, and soon discovered that a game of faro was going on. The noise disturbed him so, that he dressed himself, went to the room, and told the players, that, having tried all legal methods to break them up, and failed, he was now determined to try another plan. He thereupon seated himself at the table, and before the night was spent broke the bank. He then told the gamblers to clear out, and be more careful in future how they interfered with the court.

Once when sitting up late at night, trying a very complicated case, the sheriff voluntarily placed on the bench beside the judge a small pitcher half filled with toddy. When he had finished the toddy, the judge called to the officer, "Mr. Sheriff, fetch in some more water out of the same spring." A murder case was once tried before him. The point in the case was whether the prisoner had shot in self-defense. There was a good deal said by the lawyers about the right to shoot. The jury, intending to justify the prisoner, brought in this verdict: "The prisoner has a right to shoot." When this verdict was read to the court, the judge held up his hands in pretended alarm, and cried out, "Mr. Sheriff, don't let him shoot this way!"

A story is told of Judge Dooly and Tom Peter Carnes, another rare humorist, that fairly illustrates the statement made in the beginning of this chapter in regard to the plain and democratic character of the people who settled Middle Georgia. Dooly and his friend Carnes were traveling to court, having gone without breakfast in order to be up and on their way at an early hour. At last they reached the place where they were to get breakfast, and called for it with some show of impatience. The lady of the house, however, was in no hurry. She said that they should have breakfast the moment Charles came. So she called for Charles, blew the horn for Charles, and finally sent for Charles. When Charles put in an appearance, the two travelers found that he was a big negro, so black and fat that he fairly glistened when the sun shone on him. Naturally Dooly and Carnes were surprised They were still more surprised when the negro's mistress said in a coaxing tone, " Now, Charles, I do wish you would sit down and let the gentlemen eat, as they are in a hurry to go to court." Charles didn't like so much company; but he finally sat down to the table, on which there was a big bowl of clabber, three "hunks" of corn bread, and three pewter spoons. " Now, Charles," said the woman, "do eat, and then the gentlemen will begin." Making the best of the situation, and somewhat enjoying the humor of it, Dooly and Carnes sat down at the table and began to eat. Carnes shook his big spoon at the negro, and cried out, " Now, Charles, you must spoony on your own side;" and he kept on warning him, "Spoony on your own side, Charles, spoony on your own side." The two lawyers ate until Charles's spoon began to make raids on their side of the bowl, and then

they abandoned the feast to him and went on their way.

A landlord of a hotel, having heard some of the lawyers, among them Judge Dooly, bragging about the toothsomeness of a baked pig they had tasted, probably at Milledgeville during the session of the Legislature, concluded that he would surprise and please them by having something in that line himself. He was either ignorant or ill-advised; for, instead of baking a suckling pig, he roasted a half-grown pig, stuffed him, put an apple in his mouth, and stood him upon his stumps in a dish. In those days the seat of honor at the head of the hotel table was reserved for the judge of the court. At the head of the table Mr. Pig was placed, facing Judge Dooly's seat. The judge and the lawyers came in, sat down, and ate dinner in comparative silence. They were overawed by Mr. Pig. Though the carving knife lay handy, and the landlord and his wife were watching with impatience and uneasiness to see what the lawyers would say when they had tasted this particular roast pig, **no one** dared to touch it. At supper Mr. Pig was **still** standing defiantly in his place. He presided at every meal during the day following. On the morning of the second day, when Judge Dooly came to the table, Mr. Pig was in his old position. Thereupon the judge bowed to him gravely. "Good-morning, sir!" he said. "I am afraid you have lost your appetite, seeing you have not eaten that apple yet. I presume you are tired attending court. — Mr. Sheriff, you may discharge him on his own recognizance, until court in course, seeing we shall have no further use for him at this session, and return him the thanks of the court for his prompt and faithful attendance."

Judge Dooly was a member of the Clarke party; but on one occasion, when he was a candidate for reëlection to the judgeship of the northern circuit, some of the Clarke men declared that Governor Troup's warlike message was an evidence that he was mad. Judge Dooly made the comment, "If he is mad, I wish the same mad dog that bit him would bite me." This happy remark came to the ears of the Troup men in the Legislature, and it so pleased them that they put an end to all opposition to the judge in the election.

Judge Dooly was one of the most charitable of men. He once refused to give alms to an unfortunate woman in Savannah, and the refusal haunted him all his life He declared that it taught him never to let Satan cheat him out of another opportunity to help the unfortunate; that he had determined to err on the safe side ever after.

Just before he died, a friend called to ask after his condition. His reply was that he had a bad cold without any cough to suit it. And so, humor bubbling from his lips to the last, there passed away, on the 26th of May, 1827, the rarest humorist that Georgia, the especial mother of humorists, has ever produced. Judge Dooly had a humor that was as illuminating as it was enlivening. It stirred to laughter or it moved to tears, according as this wonderful man chose to direct it.

A great deal of the humor that originated in Georgia has been printed in books. We find it in Judge Longstreet's "Georgia Scenes," in Major Jones's "Travels," in Colonel Richard Malcolm Johnston's "Stories of Georgia Life," and in other volumes that have attracted public attention. But the best of it has been lost. It originated when the lawyers were riding about on horseback or in buggies from court to court, and tradition has only preserved a small part of it.

SLAVERY AND SECESSION.

THE dispute over slavery, which had been going on for many years, grew furious in 1850; and its fury increased until, in 1860–61, it culminated in the secession of the Southern States from the Union. Some of those who have written the history of the secession movement contend that slavery had little or nothing to do with the matter; that the South seceded because the North had refused to grant her people their rights guaranteed under the Constitution. This is true as far as it goes; but the fact remains, that secession and the war grew out of the efforts of the abolitionists of the North, and those who sympathized with them, to keep slavery out of the Territories, and to prevent the new States then forming from becoming slave States. There is no doubt that these efforts were illegal and unconstitutional; and yet, in the minds of those who made them, constitutionality was not a sufficient excuse for slavery, which, whatever might be its political status, was morally wrong: that is to say, they believed that such a wrong as slavery could not be justified by paper constitutions and the like. Some of the more extreme abolitionists of the North were just as ready to secede from the Union that recognized slavery as the Southerners were to break up a Union whose constitutional guaranties meant nothing.

It must be borne in mind that the antislavery movement began in the South. While slavery was in full
blast both North and South, Thomas Jefferson, the
greatest political leader the South has ever produced,
was at the head of an emancipation movement, and in
all parts of the South there were men whose minds
revolted at the possibilities that swarmed about human
slavery. Georgia was the only one of the Original
Thirteen Colonies in which slavery was prohibited, and
we have seen how this prohibition was repealed at the
demand of the planters. Seven Northern States, finding slavery unprofitable, abolished the system, and a
majority of the slaves were sold to the Southern States.
But the emancipation movement went on in the South.
There were more than fifty thousand free negroes in
Virginia in 1856, and there were a great many in
Georgia. A number of planters in Georgia, the most
prominent among them being Alfred Cuthbert, eman-
cipated their slaves, and arranged to send them to
Liberia.

Nevertheless the invention of the cotton gin did more
to strengthen the cause of slavery than all other events
combined. It became more profitable than ever to own
slaves; and in this way, and on this account, all the
cotton-growing States became interested in the system.
They had the excuse not only that slavery was profitable, but that self-interest combined with feelings of
humanity to make it a patriarchal institution. And
such, in fact, it was. It is to the glory of the American
character and name, that never before in the history of
the world was human slavery marked by such mildness,

such humanity, as that which characterized it in the United States.

But all such considerations as these, as well as the moral objections to slavery of any sort, humane or cruel, were lost sight of in the great controversy that grew so furious in 1850. In that controversy some of Georgia's ablest men took part, — men who were famous as statesmen all over the country. There were Alexander H. Stephens, who afterwards became the Vice-President of the Confederacy; Robert Toombs, whose fiery and impetuous character and wonderful eloquence made him a man of mark; Howell Cobb, who was speaker of the House of Representatives; Herschel V. Johnson, who was a candidate for Vice-President on the ticket with Stephen A. Douglas in 1860; Benjamin H. Hill, who was just then coming into prominence; and Joseph E. Brown, whose influence on the political history of the State has been more marked than that of any other individual.

The controversy growing out of the slavery question became so warm that it led to the breaking-up of parties in 1850. Stephens and Toombs, who had been Whigs, united with Howell Cobb, who was a Democrat. Other Southern Whigs united under the name of the American party. At the North the Whigs either joined the Republican party or united with the American party. The spirit of disunion was rampant in all parts of the South. In Georgia the Legislature had called a State convention, and a great effort was made by some of the politicians to commit the State to secession. Both Toombs and Stephens were strong Union men, and they opposed the spirit and purpose of the call for the convention. The speeches that Toombs had made in Congress were garbled by the newspapers, and he was made to appear as favoring immediate secession. He made short work of that scheme, however. He returned to Georgia in the fall of 1850, and immediately began one of the most extraordinary campaigns that has ever taken place in the State. He was in the prime of life. His fiery energy, his boldness, his independence, and his dauntless courage, were in full flower. He took issue with what seemed to be the unanimous sentiment of the State. He declared that the call for the convention had dishonored the State. He sent out a ringing address to the people, urging the South to stand by the Constitution and the laws in good faith.

By the time the convention was held, the efforts of Toombs, supplemented by those of Stephens and other conservative men, had turned the tide of disunion. Whigs united with Democrats. When the returns of the election were made known, it was found that a large majority of the members were for the Union. "With no memory of past differences," said Toombs, "careless of the future, I am ready to unite with any portion or all of my countrymen in defense of the integrity of the Republic." So it was that the convention met, and adopted what is known in our political history as "The Georgia Platform." This platform said that Georgia held the American Union secondary in importance to the rights and principles it was bound to perpetuate; that, as the Thirteen Colonies found union impossible without compromise, the thirty-one of that day would yield somewhat in the conflict of opinion and policy, to preserve the Union; that Georgia had maturely considered the action of Congress in adopting the compromise measures, and, while she did not wholly approve that action, would abide by it as a permanent adjustment of this sectional controversy; that the State would in future resist, even to the disruption of the Union, any act prohibiting slavery in the Territories, or a refusal to admit a slave State into the Union.

Thus the Union was saved in 1850 by the very man who had been charged with trying to break it up. The eyes of the whole South were turned to Georgia during that campaign; and when the people, under the leadership of Toombs, Stephens, and Howell Cobb, voted to save the Union, the tide of disunion was turned everywhere. The Georgia platform was made the platform of the constitutional Union party in the Southern States. In Mississippi, Henry S. Foote, the Union candidate, defeated Jefferson Davis for governor. The action of Georgia strengthened the Union sentiment in all parts of the country.

For a while the situation was secure and satisfactory; but, in the nature of things, this could not last. The politicians were busy while the people were asleep. The Know-nothing party sprang up in a night, and divided the people again; and in Congress the slavery discussion was renewed with extreme bitterness over the bills to admit the Territories of Kansas and Nebraska as States. This controversy was even more exciting than that which resulted in the Compromise Laws of 1850. Following close upon this agitation came John Brown's raid into Virginia, and his attack on Harpers Ferry. In ordinary times this raid would have been regarded with contempt by the Southern people. It was a ridiculous affair, — the act of a man who had worked himself up into a frenzy of folly. If the people themselves had not been influenced by passion cunningly played on by the smaller politicians in both sections, poor old John Brown would not have been regarded as a murderer by the South nor as a martyr by the North. He would have been an object of pity to the sensible men of both sections.

But the state of public opinion was such at that time, that this ridiculous venture of a crazy old man was a tremendous shock to the South. It contributed more largely than any other event to alarm the people of this section, and to turn their minds to secession as a relief from, and a remedy for, such attacks upon the peace and good order of society. It was a great stimulant to those who had long been in favor of disunion, as well as to those at the North who were ready to get rid of slavery by violence. Following this raid, public opinion both North and South became so violently agitated, that the voices of conservative men could not be heard above the storm. It was the hour of the agitator and the extremist, and they made the most of it. The Democratic Convention, to nominate a candidate for President and Vice-President, met in Charleston on the 23d of April, 1860, and remained in session until the second day of May. The confused state of public opinion was shown by the turbulent division in that convention.

At a moment when the wise men of the
Democratic party, or of any party,
ought to have taken hold of affairs
and made their influence felt,
they seemed to be unequal to
the occasion. The members
of the convention could not
agree, and the body ad-
journed to meet in Balti-
more. But the division
continued and grew
wider. The differences
could not be settled.
One faction nominated
Douglas and Johnson,
and the other nominated
Breckinridge and Lane. The
result was the election of Lincoln and Hamlin as the
candidates of the Republican party.

In Georgia three of the ablest men still stood for the
Union, — Alexander H. Stephens, Herschel V. Johnson, and Benjamin H. Hill. But they were unable to
stem the tide. The vote of the State for members of
the convention that passed the ordinance of secession
showed a majority of only thirteen thousand for disunion; but Toombs, Thomas R. R. Cobb, Howell Cobb,
and others seized the advantage that events gave
them, and, in a whirlwind of passion, swept aside all the
arguments and appeals of the more conservative men.
But, of all those who were in favor of secession,
Toombs was at that time the most powerful and influ-

ential. He so managed matters in Congress as to make the secession of Georgia follow the inevitable failure of measures that he proposed in that body.

With the people of the South, and indeed with the people of the whole country, divided between three parties, the election of a Republican candidate was a foregone conclusion. Following this came secession, with all the terrible disasters of a war in which the South could not have hoped to succeed if reason and common sense had ruled. If the South had fought for her constitutional rights in the Union and under the old flag, the result might have been different. She would have had the active sympathy and support of that large and influential body of Northern men who were sincerely anxious to see the terms of the Constitution faithfully carried out. But disunion was more than these constitutional Democrats could stand. Daniel Webster had solidified their love for the Union, and no consideration of party could affect it.

The course of the South, considering all that was involved, should have been conservative; but it was not. It is perfectly well known now that Abraham Lincoln was willing to sacrifice the abolition party on the altar of the Union. He was prompt to announce his policy in this respect. But secession came, and with it came the doom of slavery. That all was ordered by Providence, it would be foolish to deny; and yet it is impossible not to regret the great sacrifice of blood and treasure that was demanded by the unhappy war that followed secession.

THE FARMER BOY OF GADDISTOWN.

IN 1857, when Bob Toombs was looking after his large landed possessions in Texas, and bringing the squatters to terms, he received a letter from one of his political friends, announcing that the Democratic State Convention had adjourned after nominating Joseph E. Brown as a candidate for governor. Toombs was traveling with a party of friends, and to one of them he read the letter. Then in a dazed way he asked, "Who is Joe Brown?" His friend knew no more about Joe Brown than Senator Toombs did, and all the way home the travelers were puzzling themselves with the question, "Who is Joe Brown?" They were destined to find out; for the convention that nominated Joe Brown for governor brought to the front in Georgia politics one of the most remarkable men the State has ever known.

Shortly after his return to Georgia from Texas, Toombs was compelled to meet Joe Brown to consult in regard to the details of the campaign in which both were interested. It must have been an interesting meeting. It was as if Prince Charlie and Cromwell had met to arrange a campaign. It was a meeting between Puritan and Cavalier. Toombs was full-blooded, hot-headed, impetuous, imperious. Joe Brown was pale, angular, awkward, cold, and determined. It was as if

in a new land the old issues had been buried. Toombs
was a man of the people, but in his own way, and it
was a princely and a dashing way. Brown was a man
of the people, but in the people's way; and it was a
cold, calculating, determined, and common-sense way.
Howell Cobb had written to Toombs to go to the aid of
Brown, expressing a fear that the nominee, being a new
and an untried man, would not be able to hold his own
against Ben Hill, who was the candidate of the American or Know-nothing party for governor. So the dashing and gallant senator sought out the new and
unknown Democratic candidate for governor, and had
a conference with him. Toombs found the young man
strangely cold and placid, and yet full of the determination that martyrs are made of. He found that Joe
Brown had already mapped out and arranged the plans
for his campaign, and the more experienced politicians
saw nothing to change in them. They were marked
by shrewdness and sagacity, and covered every detail
of party organization. This was satisfactory; but how
could the young man sustain himself on the stump
against such a speaker as Ben Hill, who, although a
young man, was a speaker of great force and power?
Toombs thought it would be better to meet Hill himself,
and he started out with that purpose; but when he
heard Joe Brown make two or three speeches, and saw
the tremendous effect he produced on the minds of the
audiences that assembled to hear him, the older cam-
paigner went home, satisfied that young Brown needed
no instruction and no coaching in the difficult art of
influencing the people and winning their votes.

The personal history and career of Joseph E. Brown should be studied by every ambitious boy in the land, especially by those who imagine they cannot succeed because they lack opportunities that money and friends would obtain for them. From 1857 to the close of the war, and after, the political history of Joe Brown is the history of the State; but that history, attractive as it is, is not so interesting as his struggle to make a name for himself in the world. Joseph E. Brown was born in Pickens County, South Carolina, and was the eldest of eleven children. His family was English. His grandfather fought manfully against the British and Tories in the Revolutionary War. His father fought under Andrew Jackson during the War of 1812, and was at the battle of New Orleans on the 8th of January, 1815.

Joe Brown was born in 1821. His parents were not so well off as to be able to send the lad continuously to school as he grew up. He had to "take his chances." He was compelled to work in the fields in season, and was permitted to go to school only when there was nothing for him to do on the little farm. He did farm labor from the time he was eight until he reached the age of nineteen, and the schooling he had received was only of the most haphazard kind.

Before he was grown, his father moved from South Carolina into Georgia, settling in Union County, near a little valley named Gaddistown. Up to this time, though young Brown was nineteen years of age, he had learned nothing but reading, writing, and arithmetic, and very little of these. He was now compelled to work harder than ever. Settling in a new country, and on new land that had to be cleared before it would yield a crop, the Browns had as much as they could do to get the farm in order in time for the planting season; and in this severe work, Joseph E., being the eldest son, was the chief reliance of the family. He had a pair of small steers with which he plowed; and when he wasn't plowing on the farm, he was hauling wood and butter and vegetables to the small market at Dahlonega, and taking back in truck and trade some necessary article for the family. In this way he learned the lessons of patience, self-control, and tireless industry that all boys ought to learn, because they are not only the basis of content and happiness, but of all success.

When Joe Brown was twenty years old, his father allowed him to seek an education. All he could do for the industrious and ambitious boy was to give him his blessing and the yoke of steers with which he had been plowing. With these young Brown returned to South Carolina and entered an academy in Anderson district. He gave the steers for eight months' board, and went into debt for the tuition fee. In the fall of 1841 he returned to Georgia and taught school for three months, and with the money he received for this he paid for the schooling he had gone in debt for. He returned to the Carolina academy in 1842, and went into debt not only for his schooling, but for his board. His patience and his untiring industry enabled him to make such rapid progress that within two years he had fitted himself to enter an advanced class in college. But the lack of means prevented him from entering college. Instead he returned to Georgia and opened a school at Canton,

Cherokee County. He opened this school with six pupils, and the number rapidly increased to sixty, so that he was able in a short time to settle the debts he had made in Carolina. He taught school all day, and at night and on Saturdays devoted himself to the study

of law. He was admitted to the bar in 1845, and was at once successful. He made no pretense of oratory; but his simple and unpretending style, his homely and direct way of putting a case, and his faculty of applying the test of common sense to all questions, were as successful with juries as they afterwards proved to be with the people; and before the people he was irresistible.

But he was not yet through with his studies. A friend advanced him the money necessary to enter the Law School of Yale; and there, from October, 1845, to June, 1846, when he graduated, he took the lead in all his classes, and had time to attend lectures in other departments of the college. He returned home, began active practice, and was soon prosperous. He became a State senator, and was afterwards made a judge of the superior courts.

When the Democratic Convention met in Milledgeville in 1857, for the purpose of nominating a candidate for governor, it had so many popular candidates to choose from, and these candidates had so many and such strong friends, that the members found it impossible to agree on a man. A great many ballots were taken, and there was a good deal of "log-rolling" and "buttonholing," as the politicians call it, on behalf of the various candidates by their special friends. But all this did no good. There was a deadlock. No one of the candidates was able to obtain a two-thirds majority, which, according to Democratic law, was the number necessary to a nomination. Twenty-one ballots had been taken with no result, and the convention had been in session three days. Finally it was decided to appoint a special committee made up of three delegates from each congressional district. It was the duty of this committee to name a candidate on whom the convention could agree. When this committee retired, it was proposed that a ballot be taken, each committeeman writing the name of the candidate of his choice on a slip of paper, and depositing the slip in a hat. This was done; but before the ballots were counted, Judge Linton Stephens, a brother of Alexander H., stated that such a formality was not necessary. He thereupon moved that Judge Joseph E. Brown of Cherokee be selected as the compromise man, and that his name be reported to the convention. This was agreed to unanimously, and Joseph E. Brown was nominated; and yet, if the written ballots had been counted, it would have been found that Alfred H. Colquitt, who afterwards became so distinguished in Georgia, had been nominated by the committee. He received a majority of one of the written ballots when they were afterwards counted through curiosity. Twenty-three years later, Colquitt, who was then governor, made Joseph E. Brown a United States senator under circumstances that aroused strong opposition, and immediately afterwards Brown aided Colquitt to a reëlection in one of the bitterest contests the State has ever witnessed.

The unexpected nomination of Brown by the convention of 1857 introduced into State politics the most potent element that it had ever known. The nomination, surprising as it was, was not half so surprising as some of the results that have followed it. At the moment the convention nominated him, Joe Brown was tying wheat in one of his fields near Canton, in Cherokee County. He was then judge of the Blue Ridge Circuit; and on the day that his name was placed before the Democratic Convention at Milledgeville, he had returned home. After dinner he went out into his farm to see how his men were getting on. He had four men cutting wheat with cradles, and he found the binders very much behind. About half-past two o'clock he pulled off his coat and ordered the binders to keep up with him. It was on the 15th of June, 1857. The weather was very warm, but he kept at work all the afternoon. About sundown he went home, and was preparing to bathe, when a neighbor, who had been to Marietta and heard the news, rode to his house and told him about the nomination, which had been made at three o'clock that afternoon. Telling about the incident afterwards, Joe Brown, with a twinkle in his eye, said that he had heard that a good many men were anxious to buy that wheat field, so as to have an opportunity to tie wheat in it while a nominating convention was in session.

The great majority of the people of the State were as much puzzled about Joe Brown as Toombs was. Either they had not heard of him before, or they had forgotten him. In those days a man who made a reputation in the Cherokee country was not known to the rest of the State for a long time. The means of communication were slow and uncertain. But the whole State found him out just as Toombs did. He was prompt to begin the campaign. Toombs had already left the Whig party, and was acting with the Democrats. Stephens had left the Whigs, but had not become a Democrat. He was an Independent. He was, as he expressed it, "toting his own skillet." Ben Hill was Joe Brown's opponent, and these two met in debate before the people on two or three occasions. It was thought at first that Mr. Hill had the advantage of the tall and ungainly candidate from Cherokee, but the end of the contest showed that the advantage was all the other way. Mr. Hill was a man of very marked ability. He was one of the few good speakers who could write well, and one of the few fine writers who could speak well. He had courage, he had wit, he had learning, he had eloquence; he had everything, in fact, to attract popular approval and entice a popular following; but somehow, and until the very latest years of his life, he fell far short of being a popular idol. He was showy and effective before a mixed crowd, he never failed to attract applause, and it was supposed that Brown was making a losing campaign; but the campaign was going just the other way. Hill, in the course of his discussion, said hundreds of things that the people applauded; while Brown said hundreds of things that the people remembered, and carried home with them, and thought over. Joe Brown was not only a man of the people, but a man of the country people; and he pleased the city people who had formerly lived in the country. The result of the campaign was that Know-nothingism was buried out of sight in Georgia. Joe Brown was elected by more than ten thousand majority, and the Democratic majority in the Legislature was overwhelming.

Although he was only thirty-six years old when he became governor, the people began to call him "Old Judgment." This was due no less to his peculiar gift of hard common sense than to his peculiar pronunciation. His speech and his ways were "countrified," and they remained so all the days of his life. His voice was not musical, and he had a peculiar drawling intonation, which, if it had been a little more nasal, would have been an exact reproduction of the tone and manner of the Down-east Yankee. He shared these peculiarities with hundreds of the descendants of the Puritans who settled in the mountains of East Tennessee and North Georgia. He had no wish for the luxuries of life; and though he lived comfortably, he never, even when by close economy he had accumulated one of the largest fortunes in Georgia, cared to live finely. He was a plain man at first and a plain man at last, always temperate, industrious, and economical.

His term of office in the governor's chair was for two years, and at the end of that time he had almost entirely remolded and refashioned his party. He had stamped his own personality and character upon it, and it became in truth and in fact the party of the people, —the common people. In his management of State affairs he had introduced the plain business methods suggested by common sense; he dispensed with all unnecessary officials; he shook off all the hangers-on; he uprooted all personal schemes: so that when the time came to nominate a man to succeed him, it was found that the people had no other choice. His party thought of no other name.

The year of Joe Brown's second nomination, as we have seen, was the year that witnessed John Brown's ridiculous raid into Virginia. The people of the South, however, thought it was a very serious matter, and the people of Georgia were not different from those of the rest of the South. Some very wise men allowed themselves to be led away by their passions. Even Joe

Brown, as Alexander Stephens once said, "tucked his judgment under the bed" for the time being. Back of the indignation created by the John Brown raid was the unconfessed and half-formed fear that the Northern abolitionists would send their agents to the South and organize a negro insurrection. Many of the Southern people remembered the horrors of San Domingo, and there was a vague and an undefined but constant dread that such a rising of the blacks would take place in the South. But there never was any such danger in Georgia. The relations between the slaves and their masters were too friendly and familiar to make such an uprising possible. The abolitionists did send agents to the South to stir the negroes to rebellion, and some of them came to Georgia, but in every instance their mission became known to the whites through the friendliness of the blacks. There was always some negro ready to tell his master's family when the abolition agents made their appearance. Still the people resented to the utmost the spirit that moved certain so-called philanthropists of the North to endeavor to secure the freedom of the negroes by means of the torch and midnight murder.

Consequently in 1859, when Joe Brown was nominated for governor the second time, the people were greatly stirred. Sectional feeling ran high. In that year began the active movement that led to secession and the civil war. If all our statesmen had been as wise as Mr. Stephens and Mr. Hill, war would have been averted. Slavery itself, in the very nature of things, was doomed. It had accomplished its providential mission. It had civilized and christianized millions of savages who had been redeemed from slavery in their own land. It had justified its own ends, and would have passed away in good time, no matter what compromise may have been made.

Mr. Stephens and Mr. Hill were opposed to secession. They were for fighting, if there must be a fight, in the Union, and this was the true policy. For a while the people of Georgia were earnestly in favor of this; but the efforts of the abolitionists to stir the negroes to insurrection, and the inflammatory appeals of some of the leading men, led them to oppose a policy which was at once just, wise, and considerate. Even Joseph E. Brown, cool, calculating, placid, and not easily swayed by emotion, became a disunionist, demonstrating once again that beneath the somber and calm exterior of the Puritan is to be found a nature as combative and as unyielding as that which marks the Cavalier.

Joe Brown was reëlected in 1859, and did everything in his power as governor to hasten the event of secession. The National Democratic Convention met in Charleston, and the meeting showed that the differences between the Democrats could not be settled; and it so happened, that, while the South was opposed by the solid and rapidly growing Republican party, the people of the South were divided among themselves. What is most remarkable, the people of the South, after making the election of the Republican candidate certain by dividing among themselves, seemed to be amazed at the result. In some instances county meetings were held in Georgia, and resolutions sent to the Legislature declaring the election of Lincoln and Hamlin "a viola-

tion of national comity." Nothing could show more
clearly that the minds of the voters were upset.

On Dec. 20, 1860, South Carolina seceded from the
Union, and the event was made the occasion for great
rejoicing by the secession element in Georgia. Bonfires
were kindled, guns were fired, and people seemed to be
wild with enthusiasm. Georgia did not secede until Jan.
19, 1861; but Governor Brown did not wait for that
event. He committed the first overt act of the war.
He seized Fort Pulaski, on the Savannah, Jan. 3, 1861.

On the 22d of January, ten cases of muskets belonging to a firm in Macon were seized by the New
York police after they had been placed on board a
vessel. Governor Brown sent a telegram to Governor
Morgan, demanding the release of these arms. Governor Morgan hesitated some time before he made any
response. Meanwhile, Governor Brown waited three
days, and then ordered the seizure of every ship in the
harbor of Savannah belonging to citizens of New York.
Two brigs, two barks, and a schooner were seized and
held by the State troops. When this seizure was made
known, Governor Brown received official notification
that the arms had been released. He therefore ordered
the release of the vessels. But when the agents of the
Macon firm made an effort to get the arms, they were
refused. Promptly Governor Brown seized other vessels, and caused them to be advertised for sale.

This was merely the beginning of those greater
events that cast a shadow over the whole country.
The farmer boy of Gaddistown was reëlected governor
in 1861, and continued to hold the office until 1865.

GEORGIA IN THE WAR.

WHEN the Southern Confederacy was organized at Montgomery, Ala., there was great enthusiasm all over the South, especially in Georgia; and this feeling kept up until the State had given to the Confederate armies a hundred and twenty thousand soldiers, twenty thousand more than its voting population. By reason of the fame and number of its public men, Georgia had a controlling influence in the organization of the new government. Howell Cobb was president of the convention of the seceded States that met in Montgomery on the fourth day of February, 1861; and it is well known that the convention itself was in favor of making Robert Toombs president of the provisional government that was there formed. Mr. Toombs, however, expressly forbade the use of his name. The Georgia delegates then concluded to support Jefferson Davis of Mississippi for president, and Alexander H. Stephens of Georgia for vice-president.

Only a few men doubted that the South would conquer the North. and among these was Herschel V.
Johnson. There was an idea abroad that one Southerner could whip a dozen Northerners. Nobody knows
how this idea got out, nor why the absurdity of it was
not plain to all ; but the newspapers were full of it, and
the speech makers insisted on it so roundly that the
people began to believe it. One orator declared that he
could take one company of " Southrons," arm them
with popguns, and run a regiment of Yankees out of
the country. Another stated that he would be willing to drink all the blood that would be shed as the
result of secession. It is said that both of these ora-
tors were asked for an explanation by their constituents
after the war was over. The first said that the reason
he didn't run the Yankees out of the country with popguns was because they wouldn't fight that way. The
second one, who had promised to drink all the blood,
said that exposure in camp had interfered with his
digestion, and his appetite wasn't as good as it ought
to be.

At this time and afterwards there was an overwhelming sentiment in favor of the Union in some parts of
North Georgia. The people of that section had few
slaves, and the arguments in favor of the protection of
slavery in the Territories did not appeal to them : consequently they were opposed to secession. There was
but one thing that prevented serious trouble between
these Union men and the State government, and that
was the fact that Joe Brown was governor. He knew
the North Georgians thoroughly, and he knew precisely

how to deal with them. General Harrison W. Riley, a leading citizen of Lumpkin County, declared that he intended to seize the mint at Dahlonega, and hold it for the United States. This threat was telegraphed to Governor Brown by some of the secession leaders in that part of the State, and they appealed to him to send troops to Dahlonega at once, and seize the mint by force. But the governor knew Riley and the people of North Georgia too well to make any show of force. He knew that any such demonstration would excite sympathy for Riley, and inflame the Union sentiment there. So Governor Brown wrote to some of Riley's friends, telling them what he had heard, and saying that he had known General Riley too long, and had too high an opinion of his good sense and patriotism, to believe the report. At the same time the governor informed the superintendent of the mint that the State of Georgia now held that institution. The superintendent said he was willing to act under the orders of the governor.

At Jasper, the county seat of Pickens County, the feeling of loyalty to the Union was very strong. The delegate from that county to the State convention had refused to sign his name to the ordinance of secession. Soon after the State had seceded, the citizens of Jasper planted a pole, and raised on it a United States flag, and kept it floating there for several weeks in open defiance of the Confederate and State authorities. This was an event to be delicately handled. The slightest mistake would have created a state of feeling in North Georgia that would have given no end of trouble during the whole war. But the Union flag floating in Pickens

County irritated the rest of the State; and hundreds of appeals were made to Governor Brown to send troops to Jasper, and have the flag taken down by force. To these appeals he made but one response, and then turned a deaf ear to all criticism. " Let the flag float there," he said. " It floated over our fathers, and we all love the flag now. We have only been compelled to lay it aside by the injustice that has been practiced under its folds. If the people of Pickens desire to hang it out and keep it there, let them do so. I shall send no troops to interfere with it."

While this wise management on the part of Governor Brown did not change the sentiments of the Union men of North Georgia, it prevented any serious outbreak, and kept them soothed and quieted throughout the war. Matters were managed differently in East Tennessee; and the result was, that the Union men of that section went into the business of bushwhacking, and created a great deal of trouble. While Governor Brown exercised authority without regard for precedent, the time and the occasion being without precedent, he was very wise and very prudent in meeting such emergencies as those that arose in North Georgia.

By the time the election for governor came on, Joe Brown had aroused a good deal of opposition. He had had a controversy with the Confederate authorities because the latter had enrolled troops from Georgia without first making a requisition on the governor. He had seized several cargoes of salt which the speculators had been holding for higher prices. There was at that early day, and all during the war, a salt famine in the

South. The farmers found it difficult to save their meat, owing to the scarcity of salt. It is a curious fact, that, when the famine was at its height, a pound of salt was worth a pound of silver. Foreseeing this famine, a great many shrewd business men had laid in large stocks of salt, storing it about in large warehouses in different parts of the State. They were about to realize immense fortunes out of the sufferings of the people, when Governor Brown stepped in and seized all the salt the State authorities could lay hands on, and prohibited the shipment of the article out of the State. The Legislature afterwards came to the support of the governor; but if the matter had been discussed in the Legislature in advance of the action of the executive, the speculators would have had timely notice, and the State authorities would have found no salt to seize.

This salt famine was almost as serious as any result of the war, and it hung over the State until the close of the contest. In thousands of instances the planters who had been prodigal of salt before the war, dug up the dirt floors of their smokehouses, and managed to extract a small supply of the costly article. The Legislature was compelled to organize a salt bureau, and for that purpose half a million dollars was appropriated. The State, in self-defense, took into its own hands the monopoly of manufacturing salt and of distributing it to the people.

The next difficulty with which the people of Georgia had to contend was the Conscription Act. This act passed the Confederate Congress in April, 1862. It had been recommended by Mr. Davis in a special message, and Congress promptly passed it. Nobody in Georgia could understand why such a law had been recommended, or why it had passed. It was the most ruinous blunder of the Confederate Government during the war. If such a law was necessary, it showed that the Confederacy had fallen to pieces. If it was not necessary, its enactment was a stupendous piece of folly; and such it turned out to be. Under the last call for troops for Confederate service, Governor Brown had no difficulty in furnishing eighteen regiments. He could have gone on furnishing troops as long as there was any fighting material left in the State; but as soon as the Conscript Act went into operation, the ardor of the people sensibly cooled. The foolish law not only affected the people at home, but hurt the army in the field. It was a reflection on the patriotism of the whole Southern population. The law was the occasion of a controversy between Governor Brown and President Davis, in which Brown, in the nature of things, had a decided advantage; for the Conscript Act wiped out the whole theory of State rights, on which the people of the South depended to justify secession. But Georgia did not stand in the way of the law. It was enforced, and the terms of its enforcement did the work of disorganization more thoroughly than the hard times and the actual war were doing it.

In March, 1863, the governor issued a proclamation convening the Legislature in special session to discuss the subject of bread. This was a very important subject at that time. In his message, the governor said that the time had come for the farmers to raise bread instead of cotton. He also laid before the Legislature the reports of the distribution of the fund of two and a half millions of dollars for the support of the indigent families of soldiers. These reports showed what havoc the war had created among the people of a State which, not much more than two years before, was one of the most prosperous in the country. The fund had been distributed among more than eighty-four thousand people. Of this number, about forty-six thousand were children, twenty-four thousand were kinswomen of poor living soldiers, eight thousand were orphans, four thousand were widows of dead soldiers, and five hundred were soldiers disabled in service. Governor Brown, out of his own barn, gave the people of Cherokee County four thousand dollars' worth of corn. These events show the straits to which the people had been reduced by two years of actual war.

It should be borne in mind, however, that the people had to fight the Union army in front, and the speculators and extortioners in the rear. Governor Brown tried hard to make the lives of this latter class entirely miserable, and he succeeded in a way that delighted the people. Wherever he could get his hands on a speculator or extortioner, he shook him up. He made many seizures, and confiscated the hoards of a great many men who had influence with some of the newspapers; and in this way life in the State was made almost as exciting as the experience of the soldiers at the front.

In 1863, Governor Brown wanted to retire from office. The strain on his health and strength had been very severe, and he felt that he was breaking down. He wanted to make Toombs, who was then a general in the army, his successor. But Brown's friends insisted that he should make the race. The public opinion of Georgia and of the whole South insisted on it. So he became a candidate for a fourth term. He had two opponents, — Joshua Hill, who had been a strong Union man; and Timothy Furlow, who was an ardent secessionist and a strong supporter of the Confederate administration; but Governor Brown was elected by a large majority over both candidates.

The war went steadily on, and during the year 1864 Georgia became the battle ground, — the strategic point. This fact the Union commanders realized very early, and began their movements accordingly. Virginia was merely the gateway to the Confederacy, but Georgia was very near the center of its vitality. This was shown by the fact that when Atlanta fell, and Sherman began

his destructive march to the sea, it was known on all
sides that the Confederate Government was doomed.
This movement, strange to say, was hastened by the
Confederate authorities.   General Joseph E. Johnston,
one of the greatest commanders of the war, was removed at a critical moment, when his well-disciplined
army had reached Atlanta.   He was ordered from Rich-
mond to turn his army over to the command of General Hood, and within a very few days the fate of the
Confederacy had been decided.   Hood at once ordered
an attack on Sherman's lines.   He was repulsed, and
then compelled to evacuate the city.   General Sherman detached General Thomas from his main army to
follow Hood on his march toward the Tennessee, and
moved across the State to Savannah.   Within a very
few months thereafter the war was brought to a close.
Colonel I. W. Avery, in his "History of Georgia," says
that on the thirty-first day of December, 1864, one
dollar in gold was worth forty-nine dollars in Confederate money.   The private soldier received eleven dollars of this money for a month's service.   He could
buy a pound of meat with his month's pay.   He could
buy a drink of whisky, and have one dollar left over.
With four months' pay he could buy a bushel of wheat.
General Toombs once humorously declared that a negro
pressman worked all day printing money, and then until
nine o'clock at night to pay himself off.   There was a
grain of truth in this humor, — just enough to picture
the situation as by a charcoal sketch.

A DARING ADVENTURE.

O N the 12th day of April, 1862, the anniversary of
the firing on Fort Sumter by the Confederates, a
passenger train pulled out of the old car shed in Atlanta.
It was a "mixed" train, being composed of three freight
cars, a baggage car, and the passenger coaches. The
train started from Atlanta at an early hour, arrived at
Marietta about daylight, and stopped at Big Shanty,
about seven miles north of Marietta, for breakfast. At
Marietta, early as the hour was, quite a crowd of passengers were waiting to take the train. This excited no
remark. There was a good deal of travel and traffic on
the State Road at that time, for it was the key to the
Confederacy — the one artery that connected the army
at the front with its source of supplies.

The conductor of the train was Captain William A.
Fuller, of Atlanta. Captain Fuller's title was not one
of courtesy. He was a captain in the Confederate
Army, on detached service. The engineer in charge of
the locomotive was Jeff Cain. Mr. Antony Murphy,
an employee of the road, was also on the train. At Big
Shanty the passengers were allowed twenty minutes for
breakfast, but the train men were in the habit of dis-
patching their meal a little quicker than this, so as to
see that everything about the locomotive was shipshape

when the conductor tapped the bell. Captain Fuller, sitting at a table near a window, had a full view of the train. He had hardly begun to eat before he saw the locomotive (the now famous "General") and the three freight cars pull out, and heard the gong sound as the cord snapped. He rose instantly and rushed from the breakfast room,. followed by Engineer Cain and Antony

Murphy. He saw the "General" going at full speed up the road with three freight cars attached. Without hesitation Captain Fuller started after the flying train on foot, followed by Cain and Murphy. Hundreds of soldiers were idling about the station. They had no idea what was taking place. They thought either that the locomotive had been carried up the track to take on or leave a freight car, or that some practical joker was playing a prank. They showed their enjoyment of the situation by laughing and cheering loudly when Captain Fuller, followed by Engineer Cain and Mr. Murphy, started after the "General" on foot.

The locomotive had been captured, and had the plan of its captors been successful, a paralyzing, perhaps a fatal, blow would have been struck at the Confederacy. The way the capture had come about was this: Early in 1862 the Federal commanders planned an advance on Chattanooga; but the fact that stood in their way was, that at various points along the line of railroad leading from Atlanta to Chattanooga, Confederate troops had been posted: consequently the moment an advance on Chattanooga was made, soldiers and war supplies could be hurried forward to the relief of the city. It was General Mitchell of the Federal army who planned the advance; and it was J. J. Andrews, an active spy in the Union service, who planned a raid by means of which it was intended to burn the bridges on the road north of Marietta, cut the telegraph wires, and thus destroy for a time the lines of transportation and communication between Atlanta and Chattanooga, and make the capture of the last-named point an easy matter. Andrews suggested to General Mitchell that a party of bold men could make their way to a station on the Western and Atlantic Railway (called the State Road because it was owned by the State), capture a locomotive, and then steam towards Chattanooga, burning the bridges and cutting the telegraph lines as they went along. Although there seemed to be small chance for the success of such a daring adventure, General Mitchell gave his consent to it, agreeing to pay Andrews sixty thousand dollars if he succeeded. To aid him, Andrews was allowed to select a number of young men who had already made a reputation in the Federal army for intelligence and bravery.

There were twenty-four men in this small expedition when it started for Chattanooga. They were under the command of Andrews, who was a tall, handsome man with a long black beard. He was cold, impassive, and had the air of one who is born to command. He was bold as a lion, and never once lost his coolness, his firmness, or his decision. He and his men pretended to be Kentuckians who had become disgusted with the Lincoln government and were making their way South, where they might find more congenial company than that of the ardent Union men who were their neighbors at home. This story was plausible on the face of it, for many Southern sympathizers had fled from Tennessee and Kentucky when the Federals began to take possession of those sections.

Andrews and his men tramped southward more than a hundred miles before they reached Chattanooga. Before going into that city, they divided into smaller squads, and all but two succeeded in eluding guards, sentinels, and patrols, and passing into the town. They left Chattanooga on a train bound for Atlanta, buying tickets for Marietta. They reached Marietta in safety, and went to different hotels for the night. They had arranged to meet again at four o'clock the next morning and take the north-bound train. Two of the men were not called by the clerk of the hotel at which they stopped: consequently they overslept; and their companions had to go on without them when the train arrived. They had learned that Big Shanty had no telegraph office, and that it was a breakfast station. At that point Andrews determined to capture the locomotive. It was not long before the brakeman put his head in at the door of the car and yelled out, "Big Shanty! Twenty minutes for breakfast!"

Andrews and his men looked out of the windows of the car as the train drew up at the station, and the sight they saw was not calculated to make them feel certain of success. Opposite the station was a field covered with the tents of soldiers, and in and around the station thousands of soldiers were loitering and standing about. When the train stopped, Andrews, the leader, and Knight, an engineer who had come with the party, rose and left the coach on the side opposite the depot, and went to the locomotive, which they found empty. They also saw that the track was clear. Andrews and Knight then walked back until they came to the last of the three box cars. Andrews told his engineer to uncouple the baggage car from the box car, and then wait for him. Knight did as he was told, while Andrews walked leisurely back to the passenger coach, opened the door, and said quietly, "Now is our time, boys! Come on!"

The men rose at once and went out of the coach. Knight, as soon as he saw them coming, climbed into the locomotive, cut the bell rope, and stood with his hand on the throttle, waiting for the word. Andrews stood near the locomotive, and motioned with his hand for the men to get into the box cars, the doors of which were slid back. All the men were now in the box cars except Andrews, Knight, and another engineer named Brown, who ran forward and climbed into the locomotive. While this was going on, a sentinel stood within half a dozen yards of the train, but he had no idea what was occurring. Andrews gave the signal to go ahead. Instantly Knight pulled the throttle valve open, and the locomotive started forward with a jerk. It went puffing and snorting out of Big Shanty without let or hindrance.

But the train had not gone very far before the speed of the locomotive began to slacken. The fire in the furnace refused to burn, and the steam was low. While the engineer was trying to discover what was wrong, Andrews ordered the men to cut the telegraph wire and tear up a rail from the track. By the time the rail had been torn up and the wire cut, the engineer had discovered that the dampers of the fire box were closed. With these open, the boiler began to make steam again, and the locomotive was soon rattling over the rails once more. It was the intention of Andrews to run the captured train on the time of the regular passenger train, so that he would have only one train to meet and pass before reaching the Resaca River, where he intended to burn the bridge. This done, it would have been an easy matter to burn the bridges over the Chickamauga. This crooked stream winds about the valleys so unexpectedly, and in such curious fashion, that the railroad crosses it eleven times within a few miles. These eleven bridges Andrews intended to burn as he went along, and then he would not fear pursuit. His success seemed to be certain.

The captured locomotive, an old-fashioned machine with a big heavy smokestack, went clanking and clattering along the road, and reeling and rumbling through

the towns, dragging after it the three box cars containing the men whom Andrews had brought with him.
After passing a station, the locomotive would be
stopped and the wire cut. When the train reached
Cassville, wood and water were running low, and a stop
was made to get a fresh supply. The doors of the box
cars were closed, and the men inside could not be seen.
The station agent at this place was very inquisitive.
He wanted to know why so small and insignificant a
freight train was running on the time of the morning
passenger train. Andrews promptly told the agent that
the train was not a freight, but an express, and that it
was carrying three cars of gunpowder to Beauregard.
The agent believed the story, and furnished Andrews
with a train schedule.

From Cassville the distance to Kingston was seven
miles, and at that point a freight train was to be passed.
When Andrews reached the place, he found that the
freight had not arrived. He therefore switched his
train into a siding to wait for the freight train, and
repeated his powder story for the benefit of the inquisitive. When the freight arrived, he saw that it carried
a red flag. This meant another train was on the road.
After another long half hour's wait, the second freight
train came in sight, and Andrews was dismayed to see
another red flag displayed. The railroad men said
another train was following. The men on the captured
train were compelled to wait more than an hour. To
those shut up in the box cars this was a very trying
time. They had no means of knowing what had happened, or what was about to happen, until Knight, the

engineer, found an opportunity to saunter by and tell them what the trouble was. At the end of an hour the long wait was over. The freight trains had passed, and the captured locomotive, dragging the box cars, went swiftly out of Kingston. A short distance be-

yond, the usual stop was made, and the wires cut. An attempt was made to tear up the track by some of the men, while others loaded the box cars with railroad ties. While engaged in this work, the men heard the scream-ing whistle of a locomotive in full pursuit. They were more than amazed : they were paralyzed. If a pursu-

ing locomotive had sprung out of the ground at their
feet with a full head of steam on, they could not have
been more astonished. They had just passed three
freight trains headed in the opposite direction, and now
here was a pursuing locomotive coming after them at
full speed, and with a full head of steam on. Making
one spasmodic effort, they broke the rail they were trying to tear up.

Reaching Adairsville, Andrews and his men found
that the passenger train had not arrived. But it was
no time for waiting. They resolved to take every
chance. The engineer had orders to send the locomotive along at full speed. He was very willing to do
this. Calhoun was nine miles away, and if that station
could be reached before the passenger train left, all
would be well; if not, there was danger of a collision.
But Andrews took all the chances. The throttle of the
locomotive was pulled wide open, and the train started
so suddenly and so swiftly that the men in the box cars
were thrown from their feet. The distance to Calhoun
was nine miles, and the train bearing Andrews and his
men made it in seven minutes and a half, — pretty
swift traveling, when it is remembered that the track
was full of short curves, and not in the best condition.

As the locomotive neared Calhoun, Engineer Knight
gave several loud blasts on the whistle; and it was well
he did so, for the passenger train had just begun to pull
out of Calhoun on its way to Adairsville. If the whistle
had been blown a moment later than it was, the passenger train would have been under full headway, and the
signal would not have been heard; but the passenger

train had just begun to move, and was going slowly. The whistle was heard, and the engineer backed his train to Calhoun again. But when Andrews and his men arrived, they found a new difficulty in the way. The passenger train was such a long one that the rear end blocked the track. Andrews tried to get the conductor to move on to Adairsville and there meet the upbound passenger train; but that official was too badly scared by the danger he had just escaped to take any more chances, and he refused to budge until the other train should arrive. This would be fatal to the plans of Andrews, and that bold adventurer made up his mind that the time had come for force to be used. The conductor was finally persuaded to allow Andrews to go ahead with his powder train. He ran a little more than a mile beyond Calhoun, stopped his train, ordered the wire cut and another rail torn up. While they were busily engaged in this work, they were both amazed and alarmed to see a locomotive approaching from the direction of Calhoun. They had only bent the rail, and were compelled to leave it and get out of the way of their pursuers.

Andrews and his men were bold and intrepid, even reckless; but the man who had charge of the pursuit had all these qualities and more. Captain Fuller was possessed of an energy and a determination that allowed nothing to stand in their way.

We have seen how Captain Fuller sprang from the breakfast table at Big Shanty, and went running after the flying locomotive. Engineer Jeff Cain and Mr. Murphy followed after. The soldiers loitering about the station laughed and cheered at the queer spectacle of a conductor giving chase on foot to his locomotive which, with a part of his train, was running away under a full head of steam. All of Captain Fuller's energies were aroused to their highest pitch, and he easily distanced his companions. He ran fully three miles, and then came upon a squad of section hands who had been engaged in repairing the track. They were now very much excited. The captured locomotive had stopped with them long enough for the men on the box cars to seize all their tools and cut the telegraph wire, being careful to take away about fifty feet, so that the wire could not be promptly joined. From the demoralized section hands Captain Fuller learned of the number of men on the locomotive, and was given reason to suspect that they were Federals in disguise. The section hands had what was then called a pole car, a small affair which they pushed with poles from point to point. It had been derailed to make way for the up passenger train. Conductor Fuller had it lifted upon the track, and then debated with himself as to whether he should go back for his engineer, Jeff Cain, who, with Mr. Antony Murphy, had been left far behind. Concluding that it would be well to have his engineer with him, Captain Fuller pressed some of the section hands into service, and pushed down the road the way he had come, going more than a mile before he met Cain and Murphy. Once on the old hand car, Captain Fuller turned and again began the pursuit as energetically as before, although he knew that valuable time had been lost. Something of their leader's energy and dauntless spirit was imparted to the men with him, and they made tolerable speed with the pole car; but, suddenly, while they were poling along at a great rate, the car tumbled from the track. They had now come to the place where the would-be bridge burners had torn up the first rail. The pursuers were not hurt by the fall. They jumped to their feet, pushed the car over the obstruction, and were soon on their way again, going even more rapidly than before. In this way the pursuit led by Captain Fuller came to Etowah Station. Here he found the old "Yonah," a locomotive belonging to the Mark A. Cooper Iron Works. The "Yonah" was a superannuated engine, but Captain Fuller pressed it and its crew into his service. The rickety old "Yonah" seemed to enter into the spirit of the pursuit, for the distance to Kingston — thirteen miles — was made in twelve minutes.

As Andrews and his men had been delayed at Kingston for more than an hour waiting for the freight trains to allow him to pass, the pursuers, led by Captain Fuller, arrived at Kingston only ten minutes after the raiders left. The tracks were crowded with these freight trains when the "Yonah" arrived, and Captain Fuller saw at a glance that the locomotive would be of no further service in the chase. He leaped from the engine, and ran about two miles to the north angle of the Rome railway, where he knew he would find the locomotive of the Rome road standing at this hour. He pressed the engine and crew into service, and again took up the pursuit of the fleeing raiders.

Andrews and his men, in the meantime, had stopped and loaded their box cars with old cross-ties and dis-

carded rails   These they began to throw out of the
rear end of their hindmost car as a measure of safety.
They did not suspect pursuit at this time, but they took
the precaution to obstruct the track in this manner.
Six miles north of Kingston the raiders stopped and
tore up several rails.   Captain Fuller rode on the pilot
of his engine, and removed such of the obstructions as
were not knocked off by the cowcatcher.

When Captain Fuller reached the point where the
rails had been removed, his locomotive was useless.
But his blood was now up.   He abandoned the engine,
and ran on foot towards Adairsville, where he knew he
would find a through freight train.   In fact he met it
after he had run about three miles, flagged it down,
reversed it, and carried it back to Adairsville.   There,
taking the engine, tender forward, with its crew, he
renewed the pursuit.   The locomotive was run at an
extraordinary rate of speed ; but Captain Fuller felt it
to be his duty to ride on the bumper of the tender, a
precarious position even when there is no danger of
obstructions.   Beyond Calhoun, Andrews and his men
stopped to cut the telegraph wire and tear up more rails.
They had pried a rail above the stringers when they
heard the pursuing locomotive, and saw it rounding a
curve half a mile away.   They scrambled into their cars
in a hurry, leaving the rail bent but not removed.
Captain Fuller saw the bent rail, but he had also seen
the game, and he allowed his engine to be driven over it
under a full head of steam.

From this point the chase was the most thrilling and
reckless of which there is any record.   Andrews resorted

to his old trick of dropping cross-ties, but he soon saw that this would not do. Then he uncoupled one of his box cars. Captain Fuller picked it up, and pushed it ahead. Andrews uncoupled another. This was served the same way, and at Resaca the cars were run on a siding. The "General," commanded by Andrews, was now forward, with one car, while the "Texas," commanded by Captain Fuller, and driven by Peter Bracken, was running tender forward, with Fuller standing on the brake board, or bumper. The locomotives were about evenly matched. Both had five-foot ten-inch drivers, and both were running under all the pressure their boilers could carry.

All thought of danger was lost sight of. The pursued had no time to hatch any scheme calculated to delay pursuit. The pursuers forgot to look for obstructions. On one side it was capture or die; on the other it was escape at all hazards. The people of the towns and villages through which the road passes knew not what to make of the spectacle. Before they could recover from the surprise of seeing a locomotive with one box car dash wildly past the station, they were struck dumb with amazement by the sight of another locomotive thundering by, tender forward, a tall man standing on the bumper and clinging to the brake rod.

They were going at a terrific rate of speed, but Peter Bracken, the brave engineer of the "Texas," knew his locomotive so well, and handled her with such a nice eye for her weak as well as her strong points, that the pursuers gradually shortened the distance between them and the raiders. The "General" was a good locomotive in its day and time, but it was in unfamiliar hands. Any locomotive engineer will tell you that a man must be thoroughly acquainted with his machine, and somewhat in love with it to boot, to get the best speed out of it, when speed is necessary.

The raiders were pushed so closely that they soon found it necessary to abandon their engine and car. Three miles north of Ringgold, they slowed down a little, and, seizing a favorable opportunity, tumbled out, and fled through the woods in all directions. It might be supposed that Captain Fuller would be satisfied with recapturing his locomotive, which was in all respects a remarkable achievement. But he had other views. He knew that there would be no safety for the road with the bridge burners at large, and so he made up his mind to be satisfied with nothing less than their capture. In passing through Ringgold, three miles back, he had noticed a company of militia drilling in an old field. So he sent word to the commanding officer by his engineer, Peter Bracken (who, with his fireman, took the two locomotives back to Ringgold), to mount his men as promptly as possible, and join in the chase of the fugitives. This message dispatched, Captain Fuller and two of his men, Fleming Cox and Alonzo Martin, ran into the woods after the fleeing raiders. Jeff Cain, the engineer of the "General," had been left with the Rome locomotive. Mr. Antony Murphy remained in the chase until the "General" was recaptured, and returned to Ringgold with the two locomotives.

All the raiders were caught and imprisoned. Andrews was known to be a spy, and he, with seven of his men

who could establish no connection with the Federal
army in any branch of the service, was hanged. Six
escaped, and made their way to the Federal lines. The
rest were regularly exchanged.

Perhaps those that were hanged deserved a better
fate. They were brave to recklessness, and were engaged in the boldest adventure of the war. Their
scheme was most skillfully planned, and courageously
undertaken, and if it had succeeded, — if the bridges
had been burned and the door of the Confederate gran-
aries closed, — the result would have been what it was
when Sherman, with a large army, and at the sacrifice
of many men and much treasure, closed the State Road
to the Confederates in Virginia.

Andrews and his men came near accomplishing, by
one bold stroke, pretty much all that Sherman accomplished in crippling the Confederates. It was only by
the merest chance that they had such a man as Captain
Fuller to oppose them. If they had arrived at Marietta
the day before or the day after, the probability is that
they would have succeeded in their daring venture.
Captain Fuller was more than the equal of Andrews in
all those qualities that sustain men in moments of great
emergency, and greatly his superior in those moral
acquirements that lead men to take risks and make
sacrifices on behalf of their convictions, and in the line
of their duty.

THE RECONSTRUCTION PERIOD.

THE people of the State had not recovered from the chaos and confusion into which they had been thrown by Sherman's march to the sea, when the news came that Lee had surrendered in Virginia, and General Joseph E. Johnston (who had been restored to his command) in North Carolina. Thus a sudden and violent end had been put to all hopes of establishing a separate government. General Sherman, who was as relentless in war as he was pacific and gentle when the war was over, had, in coming to terms with General Johnston, advanced the theory that the South never had dissolved the Union, and that the States were restored to their old places the moment they laid down their arms. This theory was not only consistent with the views of the Union men of the North, but with the nature and character of the Republic itself. But in the short and common-sense cut that Sherman had made to a solution, he left the politicians out in the cold, and they cried out against it as a hideous and ruthless piece of assumption on the part of a military man to attempt to have any opinions after the war was over. Any settlement that left the politicians out in the cold was not to be tolerated. Some of these gentlemen had a very big and black crow to pick with the South. Some of them, in the course of the long debate over slavery, had had their feelings hurt by Southern men ; and although these wrangles had been purely personal and individual, the politicians felt that the whole South ought to be humiliated still further.

The politicians would have been entirely harmless if the life of President Lincoln had been spared. During the war, Mr. Lincoln was greatly misunderstood even at the North ; but it is now the general verdict of history, that, take him for all in all, he was beyond all comparison the greatest man of his time, the one man who, above all others, was best fitted to bring the people of the two sections together again, and to make the Union a more perfect Union than ever before. But unfortunately Mr. Lincoln fell by the hands of an assassin, and never had an opportunity to carry out the great policy of pacification which could only have been sustained at that time by his great influence, by his patience, that was supreme, and by his wisdom, that has proved to be almost infallible in working out the salvation of the Union. After Lee's surrender, the interests of the South could have sustained no severer blow than the death of Lincoln. His successor, Andrew Johnson, was a well-meaning man, but a very narrow-minded one in some respects, and a very weak one in others. It is but justice to him to say that he did his best to carry out Lincoln's policy of pacification, and his failure was no greater than that of any other leading politician of his time would have been.

It would be impossible to describe the condition of the people at this time. There was no civil law in

operation, and the military government that had been
established was not far-reaching enough to restrain violence of any sort. The negroes had been set free, and
were supported by means of a "freedmen's bureau."
They were free, and yet they wanted some practical
evidence of it. To obtain this, they left the plantations
on which they had been born, and went tramping about
the country in the most restless and uneasy manner.

A great many of them believed that freedom meant
idleness, such as they had seen white folks indulge in.
The country negroes flocked to the towns and cities in
great numbers, and the freedmen's bureau, active as its
agents were, had a great deal more than it could attend
to. Such peace and order as existed was not maintained by any authority, but grew naturally out of the
awe that had come over both whites and blacks at finding their condition and their relations so changed. The

whites could hardly believe that slavery no longer existed. The negroes had grave doubts as to whether
they were really free. To make matters worse, a great
many small politicians, under pretense of protecting the
negroes, but really to secure their votes, began a cru-
sade against the South in Congress, the like of which
can hardly be found paralleled outside of our own history. The people of the South found out long ago
that the politicians of the hour did not represent the
intentions and desires of the people of the North; and
there is much comfort and consolation to be got out of
that fact, even at this late day. But at that time the
bitterest dose of reconstruction was the belief that the
best opinion of the North sustained the ruinous policy
that had been put in operation.

The leading men of the State were all disfranchised,
— deprived of the privilege of voting, a privilege that
was freely conferred on the negroes. A newspaper
editor in Macon was imprisoned, and his paper suppressed, for declaring, in regard to taking the amnesty
oath, that he had to "fortify himself for the occasion
with a good deal of Dutch courage." The wife of
General Toombs was ordered by an assistant commissioner of the freedmen's bureau to vacate her home
with only two weeks' provisions, the grounds of the
order being that the premises were "abandoned property," and, as such, were to be seized, and applied to
the uses of the freedmen's bureau. The superior officer of this assistant commissioner, being a humane and
kindly man, revoked the order.

These were the days when the carpet-bagger and

the scalawag flourished, — the camp followers of the Northern army, who wanted money and office; and the native-born Southerner, who wanted office and money. There is no doubt that the indignities heaped on the people led to acts of retaliation that nothing else could excuse; but they were driven to desperation. It seemed, in that hour, that their liberties had been entirely withdrawn. Governor Brown, who had formerly been so popular, was denounced because he advised Georgians to accept the situation. He, with other wise men, thought it was a waste of time and opportunity to discuss constitutional questions at a moment when the people were living under bayonet rule. Joe Brown's plan was to accept the situation, and then get rid of it as quickly as possible. Ben Hill's plan was to fight it to the last. There was a fierce controversy between these two leaders; and such strong expressions were used on both sides, that General Pope made them the subject of a curious letter to his commander in chief, General Grant.

General Pope seemed to be afraid that war was about to break out again, and he assumed charge of everything. He removed and appointed mayors of cities, solicitors, and sheriffs. He closed the State University because a student made a speech which was in effect a defense of civil law. After a while the general said he would reopen the institution if the press of the State would say nothing about the affair. In 1867, General Pope ordered an election to be held for delegates to a State convention. The polls were kept open five days, and voters were allowed to vote in any precinct in any county upon their making oath that they were entitled to vote. The convention met, but, in the nature of things, could not be a representative body. Thousands of the best and most representative men of the State were not allowed to vote, and thousands of other good men refused to take part in an election held under the order of a military commander: consequently, when the convention met, its membership was made up of the political rag-tag-and-bobtail of that day. There were a few good men in the body, but they had little influence over the ignorant negroes and vicious whites who had taken advantage of their first and last opportunity to hold office.

The authority of this convention was not recognized by the State government, and this contest gave rise to a fresh conflict between the State officials and the military dictators who had been placed over them. The convention needed money to pay its expenses, and passed an ordinance directing the treasurer of the State to pay forty thousand dollars for this purpose to the disbursing officer of the convention. General Pope issued an order to the treasurer to pay this amount. The treasurer declined to pay out the money, for the simple reason that he was forbidden by law to pay out money except on an order or warrant drawn by the governor, and sanctioned by the comptroller general.

About this time General Meade was appointed to rule in Georgia in place of General Pope, and he found this matter unsettled when he took charge. So he wrote to Governor Jenkins, and requested him to draw his warrant on the treasury for forty thousand dollars. The

governor could find no authority in law for paying
over this sum, and he therefore refused. But civil government was not of much importance to the military at
that time; so, when he had received the governor's
letter, General Meade drew a sheet of paper before him,
called for pen and ink, and issued "General Order No.
8," in which the announcement is made that "the fol-
lowing-named officers are *detailed for duty* in the district of Georgia: Brevet Brigadier General Thomas H.
Ruger, Colonel 33d Infantry, *to be Governor of the State
of Georgia;* Brevet Captain Charles F. Rockwell, Ord-
nance Corps U. S. Army, *to be Treasurer of the State
of Georgia.*"

In this way the rag-tag-and-bobtail convention got its
money, but it got also the hatred and contempt of the
people; and the Republican party, — the party that
had been molded and made by the wise policy of Lincoln, — by indorsing these foolish measures of reconstruction, and putting its influence behind the outrages
that were committed in the name of "loyalty," aroused
prejudices in the minds of the Southern people that
have not died away to this day. Some of the more
vicious of the politicians of that epoch organized what
was known as "The Union League." It was a secret
political society, and had branches in every county of
the State. Through the medium of this secret organization, the basest deception was practiced on the ignorant
negroes. They were solemnly told that their old masters were making arrangements to reënslave them, and
all sorts of incendiary suggestions were made to them.
It was by means of this secret society that the negroes

were made to believe that they would be entitled to
forty acres and a mule for voting for the candidates of
the carpet-baggers.

The effect of all this was to keep the blacks in a constant state of turmoil. They were too uneasy to settle
down to work, and too sus-
picious to enter into contracts with the whites : so
they went wandering
about the State from
town to town and from
county to county, com-
mitting all sorts of
crimes. As the civil
system had been en-
tirely overthrown by
the military, there
was neither law nor
order ; and this con-
dition was very seriously
aggravated by the incen-
diary teachings of The Union
League. The people, therefore,
in some parts of the South, offset this secret
society with another, which was called the " Ku
Klux Klan." This organization was intended to prevent violence and to restore order in communities ; but
the spirit of it was very frequently violated by lawless
persons, who, acting in the name of the " Klan," subjected defenseless negroes to cruel treatment.

There is no darker period in the history of the State

than that of reconstruction. The tax payers were robbed in the most reckless way, and the rights of citizens were entirely disregarded. Even when the Republican Congress, responsive to the voice of conservative Northern opinion, turned its back on the carpet-bag government of Georgia, these men made a tremendous effort to extend their rule unlawfully. The carpet-bag Legislature was in session three hundred and twenty-eight days, and cost the State nearly one million dollars; whereas the cost of legislation from 1853 to 1862, nine years, was not nine hundred thousand dollars. In one year the State Road took in a million dollars and a half; and of this immense sum, only forty-five thousand dollars was paid into the treasury. Added to this, the road had been run into debt to the amount of six hundred thousand dollars, and it had been run down to such an extent that five hundred thousand was needed to place it in good condition.

During this trying period, Joseph E. Brown, who had been so popular with the people, was under a cloud. He had advised accepting the reconstruction measures in the first instance, so that they might be carried out by men who had the confidence and the esteem of the State; but this wise proposition brought upon his head only reproaches and abuse. The public mind was in such a state of frenzied uneasiness, the result of carpet-bag robbery and recklessness, that the people would listen to no remedy except passionate defiance and denunciation. When the name of Brown was mentioned only as a handle of abuse, Benjamin H. Hill became the leader and the idol of the people. When, in 1870, Hill issued an address declaring that the reconstruction must be accepted by the people, he was at once made the object of the most violent attacks. But Brown was right in 1864, and Hill was right in 1870, and the people were wrong. They paid dearly for their blindness in the wrongs imposed on them by men who were neither Republicans nor reconstructionists at heart, but public plunderers.

In 1871 the carpet-bag government began to totter. The governor left the State, and staid away so long that the State treasurer, a man of stern integrity, refused to pay warrants that were not signed by a resident governor. Finally the governor returned, but almost immediately resigned. In a short time the real representatives of the people took charge of affairs, and since that time the State has been in a highly prosperous condition.

"THE NEW SOUTH."

WHEN the people of Georgia had once more gained control of their State government, the political tempest that had been raging slowly quieted down. A pot that has been boiling furiously doesn't grow cool in a moment, but it ceases almost instantly to boil; and though it may cool slowly, it cools surely. There was not an end of prejudice and unreason the moment the people had disposed of those who were plundering them, but prejudice began to lose its force as soon as men had the opportunity to engage in calm discussion, and to look forward hopefully to the future. In the midst of bayonet and carpet-bag rule, the State could not make any real progress. It is only during a time of peace and contentment that the industrial forces of a community begin to display their real energy.

No State in the South had suffered so severely as Georgia during the war. She placed in the field more than a hundred and twenty thousand soldiers, — twenty thousand more than her voting population at the beginning of the war. The taxable wealth of the State in 1867 was more than four hundred and eighty-one millions less than it was in 1861, — a loss of more than three fourths. After the reconstruction period, all the

State had to show, in return for the treasure that had been squandered by the carpet-bag politicians, was a few poorly equipped railroads that had been built on the State's credit. In some instances railroad bonds were indorsed when there was no road to show for them; in others, bonds were issued in behalf of the same road under different names; so that the people lost by fraud as much or more than the amount of improvement that had been made. The "developers" who had connected themselves with the bayonet administration were much more interested in "developing" their own private interests than they were in developing the resources of the State.

But when the bayonet administration had been driven out, not less by Northern opinion, which had become disgusted with the reckless dishonesty that was practiced under the name of republicanism, than by the energetic opposition of all good citizens of the State, there came a welcome end to the bitter controversy that had been going on. The fierce rancor and prejudice that had been aroused gradually died out; so that in 1872, shortly after the State had been rescued from misrule, Horace Greeley, the great abolition editor, received in Georgia a majority of more than seventy-one thousand votes over the straight-out Democratic candidate. This, more than any other event, showed the improving temper of the people, and their willingness to make compromises and concessions for the purpose of restoring the Union and burying the spirit of sectionalism.

With this improved temper there came an improvement in the material conditions of the State. Free negro labor was a problem which the planters had to meet. For a time it presented many difficulties. It was hard to make and enforce contracts with the negroes, who had been demoralized and made suspicious by The Union League and by the harsh and unjustifiable acts of men who acted under the name, but not under the authority, of the Ku Klux Klan. But gradually all these difficulties were overcome. The negroes settled down to work, and with them a good many white men who had been left adrift by the fortunes of war and the prostration of industries. This vast change was not brought about in a day or a month, or even in a year, but was the gradual outgrowth of a bitter feeling, — the slow awakening to the fact that matters were not as bad on a better acquaintance as they had seemed. There was, of course, the negro problem; but the wiser men soon saw that this problem, such as it was, would settle itself sooner or later. The result was that everybody began to take a day off from politics occasionally, and devote themselves to the upbuilding of the resources of the State.

At first, and for several years, the negro problem seemed to be a very serious matter indeed. All the statesmen, all the politicians, all the historians, and all the newspaper editors, discussed it morning, noon, and night for a long time. Some wanted it settled one way, and some another. At the North the men who had indorsed and approved the bayonet governments of the South thought that laws ought to be passed giving the negroes social equality with the whites. Finally a compromise was made with what is called the "Civil Rights

Law," which was intended to give the negroes the same privileges at the hotels, theaters, and other public places, that the whites had. The Northern politicians pretended to believe that the efforts they were making were for the benefit of the negroes, though no doubt the majority of them knew better. Of course, the Southern people resisted the pressure thus brought to bear by the Northern sectionalists, and the result was what might have been expected. The condition of the negro was made more uncomfortable than ever, and the color line was more closely drawn. To show how short-sighted the politicians were and are, it is only necessary to call attention to one fact, and it is this: that while the Civil Rights Law has kept negroes out of public places both North and South, they ride on the street cars side by side with the white people, and it frequently happens that an old negro woman who comes into a crowded car is given a seat by some Southerner who has tender recollections of his negro " mammy."

It is worthy of note, that while the politicians on both sides were fighting the shadows that the "negro problem" called up, the problem was solving itself in the only way that such vast problems can be settled in the order of Providence, — by the irresistible elements of time and experience. A great deal of misery, suffering, and discontent would have been spared to both races, if, after the war, the conservative men of the North had either insisted on the policy that Abraham Lincoln had mapped out, or had said to the pestiferous politicians who were responsible for carpet-bag rule, " Hands off!" No doubt some injustice would have been done to individuals if the North had permitted the negroes to work out their political salvation alone, but the race itself would be in a better condition every way than it is to-day; for outside interference has worked untold dam-

age and hardship to the negro. It has given him false ideas of the power and purpose of government, and it has blinded his eyes to the necessity of individual effort. It is by individual effort alone that the negro race must work out its destiny. This is the history of the white race, and it must be the history of all races that move forward.

When Georgia, with the rest of the Southern States, had passed safely through the reconstruction period, the people, as has been seen, found themselves facing new conditions and new possibilities. Slavery had been abolished utterly and forever; and wise men breathed freer when they saw that a great obstacle to progress and development had been abolished with it. Instinctively everybody felt that here was cause for congratulation. A few public men, bolder than the rest, looking out on the prospect, thanked God that slavery was no more. They expected to be attacked for such utterances, but they were applauded; and it was soon discovered, much to the surprise of everybody, that the best sentiment of the South was heartily glad that slavery was out of the way. Thus, with new conditions, new prospects, and new hopes, — with a new fortune, in fact, — it was natural that some lively prophet should lift up his voice and cry, "Behold the New South!"

And it was and is the new South, — the old South made new by events; the old South with new channels, in which its Anglo-Saxon energies may display themselves; the old South with new possibilities of greatness, that would never have offered themselves while slavery lasted. After these hopes, and in pursuit of these prospects, Georgia has led the way. Hundreds of miles of new railroads have been built in her borders since the dark days of reconstruction, hundreds of new factories have been built, immense marble beds and granite quarries have been put in operation, new towns have

sprung into existence, and in thousands of new directions employment has been given to labor and capital.
In short, the industrial progress the State has made
since 1870 is more than double that of the previous fifty
years.

It was natural, that, out of the new conditions, new
men should arise; and, as if in response to the needs of
the hour and the demands of the people, there arose a
man who, with no selfish ends to serve and no selfish
ambition to satisfy, was able to touch the hearts of the
people of both sections, and to subdue the spirit of sectionalism that was still rampant long after the carpet-
bag governments in the South had been overthrown by
the force of public opinion. That man was Henry
Woodfin Grady. He took up his public work in earnest
in 1876, though he had been preparing for it since the
day that he could read a school history. In that year
he became one of the editors of the "Atlanta Constitution," and at once turned his attention to the situation
in which his State had been left by the war, and by the
rapacity of those who had come into power by means of
the bayonet. Whether he used his tongue or pen, the
public soon found out that he had control of that mysterious power which moves men. Whether he wrote or
whether he spoke, he had the gift and the inspiration
of eloquence; and from first to last he could never be
induced to use this great gift for his personal advance-
ment, nor could he be induced to accept a political
office. With a mind entirely sincere and unselfish, he
addressed himself to the work of restoring unity between
the North and South, and to putting an end to the sec-

tional strife which the politicians were skillfully using to further their own schemes. He was asked to be a United States senator, and refused; he was asked to be a congressman, and refused. For the rest, he could have had any office within the gift of the people of Georgia; but he felt that he could serve the State and the South more perfectly in the way that he had himself mapped out. He felt that the time had come for some one to say a bold and manly word in behalf of the American Union in the ear of the South, and to say a bold and manly word in behalf of the South in the ear of the North. He began this work, and carried it on as a private citizen; and the result was, that, though he died before he had reached the prime of his life, he had won a name and a popularity in all parts of the country, both North and South, that no other private citizen had ever before succeeded in winning.

It was Henry Grady that gave the apt name of "The New South" to the spirit that his tireless energy and enthusiasm had called from the dark depths of reconstruction. Of this spirit, and the movement that sprang from it, he was the prophet, the pioneer, the promoter. He saw the South poor in the midst of the most abundant resources that Providence ever blessed a people with, and he turned aside from politics to point them out. He saw the people going about in deep despair, and he gave them the cue of hope, and touched them with his own enthusiasm. He saw the mighty industrial forces lying dormant, and his touch awoke them to life. He saw great enterprises languishing, and he called the attention of capital to them. Looking far-

ther afield, he saw the people of two great sections for-
getting patriotism and duty, and reviving the prejudices
and issues that had led to the war, and that had continued throughout the war; and he went about among
them, speaking words of peace and union, — appealing
to the spirit of patriotism which held the Northern and
Southern people together when they were building the
Republic, when they stood side by side amid the sufferings of Valley Forge, and when they saw the army of a
mighty monarch surrender to the valor of American
soldiers at Yorktown. With the enthusiasm of a missionary and the impetuous zeal of an evangelist, he went
about rebuking the politicians, and preaching in behalf
of peace, union, and genuine patriotism.

Such was the mission of Henry W. Grady, and the
work that he did will live after him. "The New South"
will cease to be new, but the people will never cease to
owe him a debt of gratitude for the work that he did in
urging forward the industrial progress of this region,
and in making peace between the sections. He was
the builder, the peacemaker.